POWER
OF THE
BLOOD

Approaching God with Confidence

BOB SORGE

Oasis House
Kansas City, Missouri

Second Printing (2012)

For a listing of all Bob's books, go to page 153 or to
www.oasishouse.com.

POWER OF THE BLOOD: Approaching God With Confidence

Copyright © 2008 by Bob Sorge

Published by Oasis House
P.O. Box 522
Grandview, MO 64030

www.oasishouse.com

Edited by Edie Veach.

Printed in the United States of America
Library of Congress Control Number: 2008932340
International Standard Book Number: 978-0-9749664-4-1

DEDICATION

To my daughter, Katie.

You caught our baseball, Katie, which symbolizes the many things I desire to hand down to you and all my children and grandchildren. If there's anything I wish for you to catch from me, it's this: The dignity and delight of living in confident righteousness before the throne of God because of Christ's sprinkled blood.

May you have grace to pledge your heart to approach God all your days. And may you pass this heritage to all your children—natural and spiritual—that God will birth through your life and witness.

Your beauty, integrity, and consecration are stunning. You're the light of my eyes, Sweets.

So very proud,

Your dad

CONTENTS

INTRODUCTION

It is impossible to overstate the significance and power of the blood of Christ. As you walk through these pages, may your heart thrill at the magnificent privilege the blood of Christ has provided us—the exhilaration of burning in holiness at the throne of God.

At a glance, here's where this book will take you:

✤ You're going to see why the blood of Christ is so important to God, and why He responds so passionately to those who place their faith in it.

✤ You will gaze at the horror and wonder of Calvary.

✤ While the blood of Christ accomplishes many things for us, the primary focus of this book is on what the Bible calls "sprinkling with blood." It's absolutely critical that the church recover all that God intended for the sprinkling of Christ's blood to accomplish in our lives.

✤ I will share in a personal way how the Lord has brought me, through the sprinkling of blood, into new places of intimacy with Him.

✤ Your heart will burn at the glorious possibilities that open to those who devote themselves to living in holiness.

✤ As you consider the righteousness that Christ's shed blood grants the believer, you will find great boldness to approach the throne of grace with confidence.

✤ By the time you finish this book, my prayer is that you will gain an entirely fresh resolve to live every day of your life, like Jesus, in the bosom of the Father (John 1:18).

Chapter 1

HOW GOD FEELS ABOUT *the* CROSS

If you want to know what someone feels most passionately about, ask them about their highest joys and deepest sorrows. Their cheeks will flush; their eyes will flame; their words will tumble; their face will light up animatedly. Not only do they feel deeply about it, they remember every detail. That's because the stronger the emotions, the stronger the memories. Emotion-laden events and experiences, whether joyful or sorrowful, constitute the basis for some of our most passionate convictions, values, and opinions.

In the same way, if you want to know what God feels most strongly about, talk to Him about His highest joys and deepest sorrows. *I am persuaded there is nothing God feels more strongly about than the cross of His Son.* While God has known many sorrows (Isaiah 53:3), there was one that eclipsed all others. Never has anything torn and lacerated the infinite depths of God's heart as deeply and severely as the crucifixion of His beloved Son. And He'll never forget.

Look at His cross and all you see is blood. Blood on His scalp, blood on His face., blood on His neck, blood on His shoulders, blood on His arms, blood on His hands, blood on His back, blood on His chest, blood on His legs, blood on

His feet, blood on His cross, blood on the ground. It was a spectacle of blood.

And then came waves of divine wrath as the deeply offended God unleashed upon His Spotless One the punishment for our sins. As the Son endured the barrage of fiery indignation, creation itself turned dark at noonday because of the terror. None of us knows just how astronomical the pain of God was during those interminable hours of what Thomas Dubay calls, "consummate splendor in monstrous horror."

WHEN YOU COME TO THE CROSS, YOU'RE GETTING GOD AT HIS HIGHEST PASSION.

It's because of the intensity of the suffering of the Trinity during the crucifixion that that event stands out, far and above all others, as God's most memorable event ever. Because of the pain He and His Son endured, God has deeper convictions and stronger opinions about Calvary and what it accomplished than virtually any other topic.

Come to the cross and you find a God who is inflexible regarding alternatives, dire in consequences for those who reject it, lavishly extravagant toward those who receive it, and immediately responsive to those who reach for it. Why? Because when you come to the cross, you're getting God at His highest passion.

Jesus' Abandonment Left God Undone

During His crucifixion, Jesus had dove's eyes for His Father. By that I mean He had eyes for His Father only. (Doves have no peripheral vision.) Jesus' preoccupation with His Father during His suffering is revealed in the way He directed four of His seven cross utterances to His Father.

"'Father, forgive them, for they do not know what they do'" (Luke 23:34).

"'My God, My God, why have You forsaken Me?'" (Matthew 27:46).

"'I thirst!'" (John 19:28).

(No, Jesus was not saying to His tormentors, "I am thirsty, please get Me a drink of water." He was saying to His Father, "Abba, I thirst for You, I long for You, You are My source, My life, My all, and I'm desperate for You.")

"'Father, "into Your hands I commit My spirit"'" (Luke 23:46).

The majority of His seven sayings on the cross were addressed to His Father. Why? *Because the only way Jesus could endure the horror of Calvary's torment was by fastening His focus on His Father.*

It's at the zenith of Calvary's sufferings that I imagine the Father saying to the Son, "Turn your eyes away from Me, for they have overcome Me" (Song of Solomon 6:5). In other words, "Son, why are You looking at Me like that? Here I am, pouring on You the bitter cup of My wrath against mankind's sin, and there You are, standing on the nail, lifting Your lovesick eyes to Me, and giving Me Your love. I am overwhelmed by Your unparalleled devotion. Look away from Me! The look of your eyes is too much for Me, it's more than I can bear!"

I suppose the Son answering, "But Abba, where else can I look? You alone are My life. You are My purpose, My sustenance, My universe. I have nowhere else to turn. Even though You are slaying Me, I will always trust You."

Again, I imagine the Father's response, "Son, I am utterly overwhelmed by Your love. I am crushing You and still You are loving Me. Turn your eyes away from Me, for they have overcome Me. Your love has ravished My heart. As surely as I live, I am Yours forever!"

Calvary shook heaven to the core. God was undone. Jesus' fixation on His Father during His suffering moved God's heart to its very foundations. Could it be that God's heart has not yet recovered?

It Seemed To Last Forever

There's a Scripture that says, to God a day is as a thousand years (2 Peter 3:8). There was one day that, to God, seemed to last a thousand years. It was the day His beloved Son hung on the cross. That day went on...and on... and on...and on. It *never* seemed to stop.

And then the verse goes on to say, to God a thousand years is as a day. To us, Christ's crucifixion happened 2,000 years ago; but to God, it happened just a couple days ago.[1]

God has not forgotten even a modicum of the torments of Calvary. The cross is as fresh today in God's mind as the moment it happened.

The cross was intense not only in its horrific suffering but also in its interminable duration. The pain just never seemed to stop. The nightmare seemed to stretch on for a thousand years. When you see how violent the torment was, and how long it lasted, you understand why God feels so deeply about it.

How could the Father do it? How could He take the fierceness of His judgment against sin and pour it upon the Darling of His bosom? How could He watch His beloved Son writhe on the cross and not cease the horrific onslaught of everlasting wrath? Wasn't there a point where

---

1   Jesus is described in His present glorified state as "a Lamb as though it had been slain" (Revelation 5:6). That's because Christ's sacrifice is as fresh in God's mind as if it happened just moments ago.

He said to Himself, "I can't do this anymore"?

There *had* to come a point where the Holy Spirit stepped in and said, "Abba, I will help You. You can do it. You can pour out the fullness of Your wrath upon Your Son. You can empty the vial to the bottom. You can do it."

There *had* to come a point where the Holy Spirit came alongside the Son and said, "Jesus, I will help You. You can do it. You can drink the cup of the Father's wrath. You can drain the cup to its very dregs. I am with You; You can do it."

The work of Calvary was completed only through the enabling power of the Holy Spirit. This is what we see in Hebrews 9:14, "How much more shall the blood of Christ, who *through the eternal Spirit offered Himself without spot to God*, cleanse your conscience from dead works to serve the living God?"

THE CROSS IS AS FRESH TODAY IN GOD'S MIND AS THE MOMENT IT HAPPENED.

Jesus needed an angel to get through Gethsemane (Luke 22:43), but He needed the Holy Spirit Himself to get through Calvary (Hebrews 9:14).

The sacrifice of Calvary was so utterly terrifying that it could be accomplished only through the empowerment of the Holy Spirit. Such extreme measures necessitated the joint labors of all three Persons of the Godhead. The extremity of the horror became the stark backdrop against which the radiance of this "great salvation" blazes with unrivaled magnificence.

Faith In The Blood Unlocks Heaven

The blood of Christ means as much to God right now as it did the moment it was shed. It's as fresh and atoning today as it was 2,000 years ago. Every glance at Christ's blood produces unfathomable emotions within the breast of God because it reminds Him of His Son's extreme devotion and the massive work of redemption that His blood purchased. This is why faith in the blood is so powerful.

When you invoke the blood of Christ, you unlock the infinite passions of the eternal God. Believe in Christ's blood and the heart of Abba Father turns seemingly inside-out as He eagerly lavishes upon you His glorious favor. He opens the storehouses of heaven for those who look to the blood because He honors those who honor that which is most precious to Him.

There are two groups for whom the Father has extreme convictions: Those who receive the blood of the cross, and those who reject it. Invoke the blood and you are instantly as rich as Jesus Christ Himself; spurn the blood and you remain under everlasting condemnation. Because when it comes to the cross, He feels that strongly about it.

How Valuable Is The Blood Of Christ?

You know the value of something based upon what someone will pay for it. If, for example, someone is willing to give you $10,000 for your car, that amount tells you what kind of value they place on your car. The same principle holds true with the price of your redemption. You know how valuable you are to God by looking at what He was willing to pay to redeem you. *God paid the most astounding price—the blood of Jesus—to get you.* Now that you know how much He paid to procure your loyalties, you also know how valuable you are to Him. You are more valuable to God than the universe itself!

YOU KNOW HOW VALU-ABLE YOU ARE TO GOD BY LOOKING AT WHAT HE WAS WILLING TO PAY TO REDEEM YOU.

Furthermore, you know how valuable something is according to what can replace it. If your house, for example, can be replaced with $150,000, that sum becomes the measurement of how valuable your house is. The same principle holds true with the price paid for your redemption (which was the blood of Christ, 1 Peter 1:18-19). To estimate how valuable the blood of Christ is, we must consider what can replace it.

What *can* replace the blood of Christ? What can do what the blood did? What else, besides the blood, can cleanse your sins, wash away your guilt, and present you before God faultless and with great joy? Search the universe over, from eternity past to eternity future, and you reach but one conclusion: *The blood of Christ is irreplaceable!*

That's why we rightly say that the blood of Christ is the most valuable commodity in the entire universe. When the Second Person of the Trinity took on a human frame and became flesh, human blood pumped through His veins.[2] Then, when that blood was shed at Calvary, it was the blood of God that dropped to the ground. It was the blood of God that was carried to the mercy seat of the altar in heaven. It is the blood of God that stands today in the presence of God and cries on your behalf something better

---

2   The scriptural evidence is far from conclusive, but it seems possible that our resurrected bodies will be sustained by a means other than blood. After His resurrection, Jesus claimed to have "flesh and bones" (Luke 24:39), He did not claim to have blood. Paul asserted that "flesh and blood cannot inherit the kingdom of God" (1 Corinthians 15:50) because, as he went on to say, blood is associated with corruption, but the glorified body is incorruptible. Additionally, when John saw the resurrected Christ, he said that "His head and hair were white like wool" (Revelation 1:14). It's not only that His hair was white, but His head also. A white head could suggest the absence of blood. Furthermore, Hebrews 2:14 says that Christ "shared" in "flesh and blood"; the past-tense "shared" opens the possibility that He no longer has blood. If my speculation here is accurate, and the resurrected body of both Jesus and the saints does not have blood, it would further accentuate the uniqueness of God having blood for only 33 years—blood that was shed in a manner that cannot possibly be repeated ever again.

than that of Abel's blood. Abel's blood cried, "*Vengeance!*" Christ's blood cries, "*Forgive them! Accept them! Exonerate them! Justify them!*"

Never again will God have blood. If God's blood was to be shed, it had to happen during that brief window of time when Christ lived on the earth. One reason God's shed blood can never be replaced is because God will never again have blood.

No amount of money can replace Christ's blood. Gather the cumulative wealth of all the nations into a great heap, and still you don't have enough currency to purchase even one drop of Christ's shed blood.

If you owned our entire solar system and could present it to God as payment, it would not be enough to purchase a droplet of Christ's shed blood.

The soul of man is extremely valuable before God, being more valuable than all the money in the world (Matthew 16:26). But even if you laid your precious soul down at the feet of God, you could not purchase a single drop of Christ's shed blood with the sacrifice of your soul.

As the rarest treasure in creation, *the blood of Christ is irreplaceable!*

Revel in the glory of this sublime truth, dearly beloved of God: *You have been purchased by God with the most valuable thing in the entire universe.* His desire for you was so intense, so astronomical, that He paid the highest price to get you. "Behold what manner of love the Father has bestowed on us, that we should be called children of God!" (1 John 3:1).

O blessed blood of Christ!

Blessed be the Lamb of God who shed His blood for the sins of the world. And blessed be the God and Father of our Lord Jesus Christ who conceived such a lavish gift for mankind.

Chapter 2

LOYALTY *to the* BLOOD

There is nothing more important to God than the cross of Jesus. And the primary feature of that cross is the shed blood of the Lamb. God the Father is intensely loyal to His Son who laid His life down unto death, and when you place your faith in the blood of Jesus, you are touching the Father's heart in His most tender place.

When you demonstrate your loyalty to the blood by believing in the cross of Christ and invoking the blood of Jesus over your life, the Father takes the full measure of His loyalty to His Son and sets that same love upon you. *The Father loves you with the same infinite passions with which He loves His dearly beloved Son.*

Why should you be surprised at the extravagant, unconditional affections of the Father for you? You have the blood of Jesus upon you!

The declaration of Scripture about this is absolutely stunning. The Bible says that when we are under the blood of Christ, God the Father no longer prefers His firstborn Son over us, but He accepts and loves us equally with the same measure with which He loves His only begotten Son. You are as loved as Jesus!

Jesus was the one who articulated this truth in its clearest terms: "'...that the world may know that You have...loved them as You have loved Me'" (John 17:23).

Just how *does* the Father love Jesus? The answer is so vast that we will gratefully have an eternity to explore the depths of this holy love. When, before the foundations of the earth, the Son surrendered to the Father's will to serve as the Lamb who would take away the sin of the world, the heart of the Father exploded in infinite affections for His only Son.

As uncreated God, the Son was able to receive and reciprocate the fiery affections of His Father. However, in becoming the Lamb, the Son would of necessity empty Himself of some of His privileges to take on, forever, the confines of a human body. By becoming flesh, Jesus submitted to the limitations of a human body. When creating the human frame, therefore, I can imagine the Son saying to the Father, "Abba, I want Us to create man with the ability to love as deeply as We love. Because when I take on human flesh, I don't want to be diminished in My ability to love You."

I suppose the Father answering, "Son, I feel exactly the same way about this. Therefore, let's infuse into Adam's being the ability to experience a full and complete range of emotions, from severe sorrow to extravagant joy and love. In terms of his emotional chemistry, We'll make him exactly in Our image."

When God created Adam, a body was prepared for him that would suit the Son of God Himself. This is why you have such incredible capacities to love God. Your frame was created with Jesus' humanity in mind. Little wonder David said we are "fearfully and wonderfully made" (Psalm 139:14). God made us *fearfully* with the capacity to suffer horrific pain; and He made us *wonderfully* with the capacity to enjoy exhilarating pleasure. We have the capacity to love and enjoy God at levels no other creation, including even the angels, has been given.

When we realize how Jesus not only said "yes" to the cross in advance, but also prepared a body at Adam's creation that would enable Him to suffer horrifically, our only fitting response is that of loving adoration and honor.

Honoring The Cross

Suppose someone decided that he or she wanted to honor the cross—what should he do? Should he weep in empathy and sing doleful songs?

No. Jesus didn't die to get your pity. Even He Himself said, "'Do not weep for Me'" (Luke 23:28).

The greatest way you can honor the bloodied sacrifice of Calvary is by placing your faith in the redemption Jesus purchased and believe that God raised Him from the dead, unto the saving of your soul.

IF YOU REALLY WANT TO HONOR HIS SACRIFICE, YOU WILL *BELIEVE* IN THE EFFICACIOUS WORK THAT HE ACCOMPLISHED ON YOUR BEHALF AND *RECEIVE* ITS BENEFITS.

The greatest way you can honor the stripes that were laid on Jesus is by placing your faith in the punishment He bore, unto the healing of your body and soul.

If you really want to honor His sacrifice, you will *believe* in the efficacious work that He accomplished on your behalf and *receive* its benefits.

The Glory Of The Cross

The cross gives significance to the pain of the world. Without the cross, all the anguish of the human race would be considered senseless suffering. But now, all the distresses of mankind are viewed against the backdrop of the cross.

In the silhouette of Calvary's twilight, I see a God hanging there who is not removed or insulated from my suffering. This is not a God who is impervious to my pain. Rather, I see a God who has intentionally inserted Himself into my world of pain, drinking more deeply from the cup of suffering than any other human being ever has.

Consequently, no one can look at God and say, "You don't understand. You have no idea what I'm going through." To the contrary, He empathizes with our sufferings from first-hand experience. He who suffered in the body cares for all who suffer in their bodies, since He Himself is in the body also.

It's the cross that makes our Gospel universally relevant. You can take it anywhere in the world. Take the Gospel to the worst hell-hole on the planet, and you have a message to lift the lowest life. Find the most destitute, sin-scarred, addiction-bound, demon-possessed, filthy human specimen you can possibly find, and you'll find someone whom the Gospel can take up in its arms. Why? Because the One who suffered on the tree sank lower than any other person that He might raise up the chiefest of sinners and seat them at His table.

O the wisdom and glory of the cross! The blood of His cross has my fealty forever!

When I can't make sense of my journey, I go back to the cross. When I can't process my pain levels, I go back to the cross. When my wound seems incurable, I go back to the cross. When I can't see my way forward, I go back to the cross.

When it feels like He's withholding from me, I go back to the cross. Because sometimes the accuser hits me with that ancient accusation, "God's withholding from you. He could deliver you right now, but He's holding out on you." That accusation is as old as the hills. It dates all the way back to the Garden of Eden, when Satan first accused the

Father to Eve. Essentially, his accusation to Eve was, "God knows how much better you would be if you ate of the tree. That's why He's withholding it from you. He doesn't want you to become everything you could fully be." That's still one of the accuser's favorite accusations— "God's withholding from you." He's probably tried that one on you, too.

But the cross *nailed* that accusation. Because when I look at the cross, I see a God with nails in His hands, a nail in His feet, a crown of thorns on His brow, and stripes on His back. As He hangs there with arms spread wide, He says to me, "I give you My mind. I give you My soul. I give you My heart. I give you My body. I give you My strength. I give you My all. I give you My last breath. I give you My last drop of blood."

I declare to you that my God withholds *nothing* from me! He has given me His best. He has given me His all. His extravagance has empowered me, in turn, to withhold nothing from Him. He has given me His everything, and now I give Him my everything. I am His, and He is mine.

God doesn't ever have to do another thing for me, to prove that He loves me. If He never does anything for me ever again—if He never blesses me, if He never answers my prayer, if He never delivers me—the cross is enough to prove the authenticity of His undying affection. It's because of the cross that I *know* He loves me!

JESUS DIDN'T WANT TO DO THE CROSS.

And since His cross has made me so confident in love, I will *never* be silent; I will *never* relent; I will *never* let go; but I always lift my cry to my God and call on His name, until He fulfills His promise and delivers me.

Loyal To The Cross

When someone is loyal to you, you never forget. You always remember the brother or sister who supported you, believed in you, took the heat for you, and stood with you when times were tough. There's an unusual dimension of love that is manifest whenever loyalty is present. It's out of the ordinary. Whenever this kind of loyalty is demonstrated, you never forget it.

Similarly, the Father will never forget the Son's loyalty on the cross. The Father vexed His Son's soul, even unto death, and still the Son remained loyal in love. And the Father will *never* forget.

Nor will Jesus forget your loyalty to Him. When you give Him your love and serve Him regardless of the pain, regardless of the adversity, regardless of the warfare, regardless of the perplexity, He takes it personally. He calls it loyalty, and He never forgets.

THE CROSS WAS THE ULTIMATE ACT OF LOYALTY.

I will tell you why my crucified Savior has won my endless loyalty. It's because He did the cross even when He didn't want to. The cross was the Father's will, not the Son's. *Jesus didn't want to do the cross.* "Nevertheless, not My will, but Your will be done."

So why did He do it? There's only one feasible answer. He did the cross out of loyalty to His Father. The prayer of Gethsemane was not primarily an issue of *surrender*; it was an issue of *loyalty*.

It's in the Garden that I hear a Man crying, "Abba, I just need to hear it from You one more time. Since We last talked about this, have You found another way? Is it possible for this cup to pass from Me? I don't want to drink this cup. But if there is no other way, then I will drink it, Abba, for My loyalty is Yours. Above all else, I am Yours and You are Mine."

The cross was the ultimate act of loyalty.

When the Father looks at this loyalty, He says, "I will *never* forget."

When I look at this loyalty, I say, "I give my heart—the entirety of my being—to You. Since You were loyal to Your Father even unto death, that makes You *safe* to follow. So I will be loyal to You all my days."

I pledge my troth to the blood of His cross. His extravagant sacrifice has won my everlasting devotion. Now I will follow Him wherever He goes because, above all else, I'm loyal to the Lamb.

Chapter 3

THE POWER *of the* BLOOD

When we're awakened to the glory of the cross and the blood that was spilled there, our hearts reach and yearn for greater insight into what His blood accomplished. We would be lost without the blood of Calvary. The blood of Jesus is the most powerful cleansing agent in the universe!

Here are some of the ways the power of Christ's blood is made effective in our lives.

Washes Us From Our Sins

When we place our faith in Christ and confess Him as our Savior, He washes us clean of *all* our past sins! "To Him who loved us and washed us from our sins in His own blood" (Revelation 1:5).

The Bible points to this reality in several ways. It says our sins are forgiven by the blood (Isaiah 53:5; Ephesians 1:7; Colossians 1:14; Hebrews 9:22); it says we are justified by His blood (Romans 5:9); and it says we are sanctified through His blood (Hebrews 13:12).

Under the Old Covenant, sins were not completely washed away, because "it is not possible that the blood of bulls and goats could take away sins" (Hebrews 10:4).

Rather, sins were covered over by the blood of animals.
The New Covenant is far superior. The blood of Christ
does not simply whitewash over our sins; it actually re-
moves them so that He doesn't even remember what our
sins were (Hebrews 10:17).

Cleanses Our Garments

The redeemed of the Lord are clothed in linen garments
that are "white and clean" (Revelation 19:14), reflecting
the dignity to which Christ has raised us. In our former
way of life, we were clothed with filthy garments stained
by sin (Zechariah 3:3-4), but now in Christ we are clothed
in honorable robes of righteousness (Isaiah 61:10). The
fine linen we wear is said to represent "the righteous acts
of the saints" (Revelation 19:8).

THE BLOOD OF JESUS
IS THE MOST POWER-
FUL CLEANSING AGENT
IN THE UNIVERSE!

Although Christ's blood ran red,
those who cleanse their filthy garments in this crimson tide are said
to "'have washed their robes and
made them white in the blood of the
Lamb'" (Revelation 7:14).

Purchased Our Redemption

We were slaves to sin (Romans 6:20). Historically,
only the rich ever had slaves because they were always so
expensive to buy. We slaves didn't come cheap. To redeem
us, Jesus had to pay a sufficient enough price. What was
the price tag on all these human slaves?

Psalm 49:8 answers that question: "For the redemption
of their souls is costly." Talk about an understatement! To
buy these human slaves would require the *ultimate* price.
It would mean the shedding of His very own blood (Acts
20:28; 1 Corinthians 6:19-20; 1 Peter 1:18-19).

Jesus paid the price to buy us from our slavery and

make us "slaves of God" (Romans 6:22). The blood of Christ has delivered us from sin's power that once held our lives. Hallelujah! Now, instead of serving sin, we are servants of God.

Jesus is an exceedingly wise Merchant. He's not about to pay an exorbitant price for a possession that isn't worth the purchase price. When Jesus looked at us, and then at the price that was required to buy us, He calculated the cost and determined that we were worth it.

Provides For Our Healing

In looking forward to Calvary, Isaiah prophesied, "The chastisement for our peace was upon Him, and by His stripes we are healed" (Isaiah 53:5). Isaiah was pointing specifically to the scourging that Jesus would receive prior to His crucifixion. The blood that was drawn by the whips in Jesus' scourging is the basis for our healing in the New Covenant.

Peter confirmed that when he wrote, "by whose stripes you were healed" (1 Peter 2:24). Peter used the past tense ("*were* healed") because our healing was accomplished that day during His scourging. Today, we embrace His healing of our bodies as a work that has already been accomplished.

Have you ever wondered why Jesus agonized for hours on the cross? Why didn't He die a quick death, like the lambs that were sacrificed in the Old Testament? Wouldn't a quick death have been adequate for Jesus, the innocent Lamb, to atone for the sins of the world? But instead, He died a slow, torturous, agonizing death. Why? One reason is because His cross did more than atone for sins. It also paid the price for sorrows, griefs, pains, sicknesses, iniquities, and peace of mind (Isaiah 53:3-5). Through faith, we are now healed from our griefs *and* pains *and* sicknesses.

If I was healed then, I'm healed now. The blood of Jesus heals me. It is through faith in the blood of His scourging that we pray for the sick and they recover.

Silences The Accusations Of The Evil One

The devil is constantly accusing God's people, pointing out their sins and shortcomings, and telling them they are unworthy to stand before God. But we have been given a weapon to silence His accusations: the blood of Christ.

> Then I heard a loud voice saying in heaven, "Now salvation, and strength, and the kingdom of our God, and the power of His Christ have come, for *the accuser of our brethren, who accused them before our God day and night,* has been cast down. *And they overcame him by the blood of the Lamb* and by the word of their testimony, and they did not love their lives to the death" (Revelation 12:10).

Many of Satan's accusations are based on sins we have actually committed. However, the blood of Jesus is our weapon against his accusations. We receive the cleansing of His blood, stand faultless in the presence of God, and then declare to our accuser, "You have no right to accuse me of that sin because it has been washed away by the blood of Christ."

Lester Sumrall told of the time he ministered deliverance to a demonized girl in the Philippines. She only spoke a local dialect, no English. But the demon in her began to speak with pure, unbroken English. The evil spirit first cursed the Father, then the Son, then the Holy Ghost, and then the blood of Jesus—in that order. Lester observed that the way the demon cursed the blood seemed as though it believed the blood of Jesus was *alive*.[1] I am told it was C.S. Lewis who said, "On the back of Satan's neck is a nail-scarred footprint." The Lamb is the ultimate military strategist! In six hours, Jesus undid 6,000 years of the accuser's oppression over mankind.

Cleanses Us From A Guilty Conscience

The blood silences the accusations of our enemy. But he's not the only source of accusation. We also receive accusation from another source: ourselves. Our own conscience often smites us, accusing us of sin—because we're so frequently and painfully aware of our own failures.

There may be nothing more immobilizing in the believer's life than feelings of guilt. *When you feel guilty before God, you can't pray, you can't exercise faith, you can't receive healing, you can't believe for financial provision, you can't worship— you're hamstrung.* That's why it's so vitally important that we receive the provision of Christ's blood for the accusations of our conscience.

JESUS LOOKED AT THE PRICE REQUIRED TO BUY US AND DETERMINED WE WERE WORTH IT.

How much more shall the blood of Christ, who through the eternal Spirit offered Himself without spot to God, cleanse your conscience from dead works to serve the living God? (Hebrews 9:14).

The conscience is a strange, unpredictable thing. Sometimes it operates with total accuracy; other times, it misses the mark completely. It misses it during those times when we are standing justified in the presence of God but

1 H.A. Maxwell Whyte, *The Power of the Blood*, New Kensington, PA: Whitaker House, 1973, page 29.

our conscience is still jabbering away, trying to convince us that we're still unclean. When fighting that battle with our own accusing thoughts, all we need do is simply pray, "Jesus, cleanse me with Your blood," and the accusations of our conscience are immediately silenced.

The blood cleanses the conscience! Wow! It's here that we *really* see the power of the blood. No self-help effort could ever pacify one's conscience. But the blood silences the loquacious tongue of an evil conscience.

When your conscience is cleansed, you actually *feel* clean. In the technical (legal) sense, justification means that you *are* clean, whether you feel like it or not. But the blood takes it a step further and actually makes you *feel* clean. O the power of the blood!

Cleanses Us From The Defilement Of Recently Committed Sins

This cleansing happens through what the Bible calls "the sprinkling of blood."

We live in a sin-ridden, defiled world in which it's incredibly easy to get soiled—sometimes without even realizing it. Even with the most sincere efforts to live in godliness, we often become defiled simply by living in a defiled environment.

THE BLOOD SILENCES THE LOQUACIOUS TONGUE OF AN EVIL CONSCIENCE.

This is where the sprinkling of blood demonstrates its power. When we ask Jesus to sprinkle us with His blood, we are immediately cleansed from anything that might stand between us. Any distance that might have developed between us is immediately removed, and we are emboldened to wrap our arms around our Father and abide in His embrace.

The sprinkling of blood is a powerful and glorious

reality, and it is to this sublime truth that we now direct our focus.

Chapter 4

THE SPRINKLING *of* BLOOD

One of the most empowering, liberating, and revitalizing things you can do is acknowledge, on a daily basis, the efficacious power of the blood of Jesus Christ upon your life. And I want to tell you how to do it: By getting sprinkled with blood every day.

When I stumbled onto this secret, I found sprinkling with blood to be so meaningful that it has become my daily practice.

Why Get Sprinkled With Blood?

"When I was made a new creation in Christ," someone might respond, "the blood of Jesus was applied to my life and I was cleansed of my sins. I already have the blood of Jesus over my life, so why would I need to repeat that? Isn't once enough?"

Good question. It's true that when we come to Christ, the blood of Jesus redeems, cleanses, and justifies us (makes us righteous) in the sight of God, as the following verses testify:

> In Him *we have redemption through His blood, the forgiveness of sins,* according to the riches of His grace (Ephesians 1:7).

Much more then, having now been *justified by His blood*, we shall be saved from wrath through Him (Romans 5:9).

Knowing that you were not *redeemed* with corruptible things, like silver or gold, from your aimless conduct received by tradition from your fathers, but *with the precious blood of Christ*, as of a lamb without blemish and without spot (1 Peter 1:18-19).

To Him who loved us and *washed us from our sins in His own blood* (Revelation 1:5).

When we were redeemed and justified by the blood of Christ, that was a one-time work of Christ's blood that need never again be repeated. Once purchased, our justification is sure and secure. You only need to be redeemed once. One application of Christ's blood redeems you, once for all.

IN SPRINKLING, I RECEIVE HIS BLOOD *UPON* MYSELF; IN COMMUNION, I TAKE HIS BLOOD *INTO* MYSELF.

There is another application of Christ's blood, however, that is to be repeated as frequently as desired. It's the sprinkling of blood. It's appropriate to get sprinkled with blood many, many times. The sprinkling of blood does not give you the justification of redemption; with sprinkling, you're after something different.

"But I receive the Lord's Table every day," someone else might object. "Isn't that enough?"

Again, good question. Receiving the Lord's Table, even on a daily basis, is powerfully enriching, but the receiving of the cup of Communion is a different operation of the Spirit from the sprinkling of blood. When I drink the cup, I am remembering and identifying with His death. His blood becomes my drink which sustains and nourishes me. However, when I am sprinkled with blood, I am cleansed from a guilty conscience. Both operations of the blood are wonderful but distinct from each other. In sprinkling, I receive His blood *upon* myself; in Communion, I take His blood *into* myself.

"Well, then, what exactly *is* the sprinkling of blood?" Thanks for asking!

What *Is* The Sprinkling Of Blood?

The best answer is found in the book of Hebrews.

> Therefore, brethren, *having boldness to enter the Holiest by the blood of Jesus,* by a new and living way which He consecrated for us, through the veil, that is, His flesh, and having a High Priest over the house of God, let us draw near with a true heart in full assurance of faith, *having our hearts sprinkled from an evil conscience and our bodies washed with pure water* (Hebrews 10:19-22).

When we ask Jesus to sprinkle us with His blood, we are asking for a fresh application of the blood of Christ to our hearts so that we might draw near to God with a clean conscience.

How do we get our hearts sprinkled with blood? By simply praying along these lines, "Lord Jesus, sprinkle me now with Your blood." How do we wash our bodies with pure water? Water points to the word of God (see Ephesians 5:26), so we wash our bodies in the water of the word by taking time to meditate and pray in a portion of Scripture.

This passage is describing what might be termed a "spiritual shower." Just as you might grab a shower or bath in the morning to freshen up and get that clean feeling, you might also consider grabbing a "spiritual shower" while you're in the cleanup mode. How? By asking Jesus to sprinkle you with His blood, and then by washing yourself in the pure water of God's word (Scripture reading and meditation). The blood cleanses your heart, and the word cleanses your body. After you've been sprinkled with blood and washed in the word, now you're *really* ready to tackle your day!

Peter made it clear that the sprinkling of blood was more than just a one-time application of Christ's blood at our regeneration.

> Peter, an apostle of Jesus Christ, to the... elect according to the foreknowledge of God the Father, in sanctification of the Spirit, for obedience and sprinkling of the blood of Jesus Christ (1 Peter 1:1-2).

While the NKJV says "for obedience," it would be more accurate to render it "unto obedience" (KJV). The meaning of the verse is that the elect are sanctified unto the goal or end of obedience and being sprinkled. The Greek word for "sprinkled" is passive, literally "being sprinkled," which hints at a recurring process.

Peter is telling us that the purpose of our calling is that we might come into obedience to Christ and be sprinkled with His blood. These two things characterize the Christian life: obedience and sprinkling.

The Spirit sanctifies us, Peter asserts, in order to bring us "unto" obedience. The word "obedience" pretty much sums up the Christian life. It starts and ends with obedience. However, none of us lives in the perfection of 100% obedience. That's where sprinkling comes in. Sprinkling with blood is God's gracious way to cover us when we fall short of perfection. We pursue obedience with fervent resolve, and then get sprinkled with blood to cover our deficiencies.

Obedience is not a one-time event that, once fulfilled, is now behind us; rather, it is a daily, ongoing practice. The same is true for sprinkling. Obedience and sprinkling are recurring processes in the life of the believer. To the degree we fall short of perfect obedience is the degree to which the sprinkling of blood is relevant to our lives on an ongoing basis.

I do not view Peter to be presenting sprinkling as an obligatory *requirement* but as a glorious *privilege*. If Christ provided sprinkling as my means of remaining confident before God in the wake of less-than-perfect obedience, why would I ever want to neglect such a wondrous benefit?

Let me insert one qualifier here. When we're sprinkled with blood, it doesn't mean we now have license to live in compromise. We are not saying, "It doesn't matter how you live, because Jesus will cleanse all your sin with His blood." No, it *does* matter how you live. Sprinkling with blood was never designed by God as a permission-granting mechanism to give believers more boldness to sin; rather, it is God's provision for those who are wholeheartedly pursuing radical obedience.

WE OBEY HIM WITH RESOLVE AND SINCERITY; THEN, WE GET SPRINKLED WITH BLOOD BECAUSE OF OUR SHORTCOMINGS.

We obey Him with resolve and sincerity; then, we get sprinkled with blood because of our shortcomings.

Just as surely as we fall short of the fullness of complete obedience on a daily basis, even so we need to be sprinkled with blood every day. This is what John meant when he wrote, "But if we walk in the light as He is in the light, we have fellowship with one another, and *the blood of Jesus Christ His Son cleanses us from all sin*" (1 John 1:7).

So what is the sprinkling of blood? It is a fresh application of Christ's blood to the believer's heart that cleanses from all defilement or guilt of sin, purifies the conscience, and thus empowers him or her to draw near to God with confidence. And it can be invoked as frequently as desired.

The Basis For Drawing Near

Let's be real clear about this: The only basis upon which we draw near to God is the shed blood of Jesus Christ applied to our lives. As Paul wrote, "But now in Christ Jesus you who once were far off have been brought near by the blood of Christ" (Ephesians 2:13). When we're under the blood, we're as acceptable to God as Jesus Christ Himself. And the inverse is equally true. Without His blood on our lives, no one is ever accepted into God's presence, for "without shedding of blood there is no remission [of sin]" (Hebrews 9:22).

When I have had a bad day—that is, a day in which I've failed to attain full obedience—I am still able to draw near to God, despite my failures. Why? Because I can confess my sin, receive the sprinkling of His blood, and immediately draw near to God with confidence. My basis for drawing near is just one thing: the blood of Christ.

When I have had a good day—that is, a day in which I have felt victorious in my Christian walk and have done nothing to knowingly step outside the lines of obedience—I am still not qualified to draw near to God on the merit of my own righteousness. Why not? Because my own righteousness, at its height, is still inadequate to qualify me to draw near to the holiness of God. Isaiah made that clear when he wrote, "But we are all like an unclean thing, and all our righteousnesses are like filthy rags" (Isaiah 64:6). So again, even when I've had a great day of holy living, my basis for drawing near is only one thing: the blood of Christ.

My basis for drawing near to God, therefore, has nothing to do with my performance as a Christian. Good day or bad day, breakthrough or failure, joy or sorrow, exhilarated or depressed, full of the Spirit or running on empty—none of that determines my acceptability to God. I don't draw near on the basis of my personal victories, nor am I excluded because of personal defeats. I can *always* draw near to God, but only on the basis of one thing: the sprinkled blood of Christ applied to my heart.

The Blood Makes Me Righteous

Only perfect righteousness can draw near to God (Psalm 24:3-5). God will not allow defilement into His presence. To draw near to God, all defilement must be washed away. The only thing that cleanses sin is the blood of Christ. It makes us clean and righteous in the sight of God.

When God sees the blood of Christ on our lives, He ascribes to us the performance record of Jesus Christ. Jesus alone was able to live the kind of righteous life that satisfies God. When under the blood, God sees us "in Christ," and Christ's scorecard becomes ours. As 2 Corinthians 5:21 tells us, "For He made Him who knew no sin to be sin for us, that we might become the righteousness of God in Him." The blood has the power to make us the very righteousness of God in Christ.

The blood satisfies God's righteous standard so that we do not merely receive a reluctant hearing at the throne; rather, we receive an enthusiastic embrace from a loving Father who has been beckoning and yearning for intimacy with us.

The Purpose Of Sprinkling

There is one primary reason to get sprinkled with blood. Hebrews specifies it clearly.

> Therefore, brethren, *having boldness to enter
> the Holiest* by the blood of Jesus, by a new
> and living way which He consecrated for us,
> through the veil, that is, His flesh, and having
> a High Priest over the house of God, *let us
> draw near* with a true heart in full assurance
> of faith, having our hearts sprinkled from an
> evil conscience and our bodies washed with
> pure water (Hebrews 10:19-22).

The purpose of sprinkling is to draw near to God.

The blood doesn't automatically bring me near. The blood only *qualifies* me to draw near. After I have been sprinkled, I must then take the next step and draw near. It's theoretically possible to get sprinkled with blood and then not give God another thought for the rest of the day. But if I do that, I have totally neglected the entire purpose of sprinkling.

The purpose of sprinkling is not to feel clean. True, the sprinkling of blood cleanses the conscience and gives us a clean feeling before God. But some believers make the mistake of getting their conscience clean through sprinkling and then taking off and going about their day. Sprinkle, sprinkle, then VAMOOSE—they're gone. They're clean, but they've missed the whole point! The purpose of sprinkling is not merely to get clean, but to draw near.

THE PURPOSE OF SPRINKLING IS TO DRAW NEAR TO GOD.

Instant Intimacy

If you're like me, you don't have room in your day to take an extra 15 minutes in the morning just to push and fight your way through to intimacy with God. You need "instant intimacy"—a way to approach God that places you immediately in His presence and embrace. *The key to instant intimacy is found in the sprinkling with blood.*

Here's how I do it. I simply pray, "Lord Jesus, sprinkle me now with Your blood," and I believe that He does it right then and there. Because of the blood, I realize in that instant that I have full access to the throneroom. So I see myself (with the eyes of faith) coming immediately and boldly to the throne of grace and stepping into the courts of the King. I make one simple petition and BOOM, I'm there, in the immediate presence and glory of Almighty God.

"It's me again, Lord!"

I'm able to stand before Him with confidence, not because my past 24 hours were spiritually spectacular, but because I am covered with the precious blood of the Lamb. His blood gives me the right to step into the command center of the universe. Now I sit with Christ in heavenly places, in His place of advantage, seeing with His perspective, sharing in His authority, and wrapped in the embrace of His eternally fiery affections.

What is the nature of this intimacy? To speak of it, I need to point to the intimacy of the living creatures at the very throne of God.

There are four creatures who are distinguished, above all the angels and cherubim, as having the closest proximity to the throne. When John was shown these "living creatures" (Isaiah called them "seraphim" or "burning ones"), he was struck by their stunning appearance (for example, they had eyes all around and within their being) and by their unending eulogy, "'Holy, holy, holy, Lord God Almighty, who was and is and is to come!'" (Revelation 4:8). But he was also struck by their immediacy of presence at the throne. John describes them as being "in the midst of the throne, and around the throne" (Revelation 4:6).

Notice they're not *on* the throne; they're *in* and *around* the throne.

No one has closer access to the throne than these living creatures—no one, that is, except the one who is sprinkled with blood. Through the blood of Christ, we are not merely brought *to* the throne, or *around* the throne, or even *in* the throne; we are brought into the very *bosom* of the One on the throne (John 1:18). When we come to God, we step past angels, past cherubim, and even past the living creatures, into a place of intimacy that is shared only by the Son of God: the bosom of the Father!

The sprinkling of blood brings us instantly into the intimacy of the Father's bosom. Don't be surprised if, once you're there, you find yourself echoing the glorious refrain, "Holy, holy, holy!"

Bringing My Issues Into The Throneroom

I'm so glad that I don't have to clean up my performance record before drawing near to God. If I had to get my act together *first* before drawing near, I would *never* get there! Here's the wonder and power of the blood of Christ: *His blood qualifies me to come into the inner sanctum of God's glory even when I have not yet fully perfected the Christian walk.*

I have likened God's glory to radiation, and the sin-issues in my life to cancer. Coming into God's presence is like getting cancer radiation treatments. Without the blood, I would never be able to bring my cancerous issues into the light of His radiating glory. But now, because I'm sprinkled with blood, I can expose my cancerous heart to the radiation of His fiery presence—and stay there.

It's not as though Christ's shed blood has dumbed down God's standards, so that He now allows all kinds of trash into His courts. God's standards for what can enter

His presence have never changed. Here's what Christ's blood has accomplished for us: It has elevated our status and qualified us to meet God's righteous, holy standards. Now, with the blood covering us, we are fully acceptable to God and pulled into His embrace. He sees us as already perfected in Christ, with Christ's righteousness credited to our account. In the eyes of God, the only thing that stands between us and full maturity is *time*. And time is no problem for God; it doesn't limit Him in any way. To Him, our maturity is as good as done. We're acceptable to Him *now*. And it's here, cradled in the arms of our Beloved, that we are transformed "from glory to glory" (2 Corinthians 3:18).

The presence of God is the place of change. Getting into God's presence is our only hope for change. If we're disqualified from drawing near, we're consigned to hopeless failure. Thus, drawing near to God becomes our highest priority in life. Little wonder we're so grateful for the blood of Christ! The blood of Christ is our sole authority in drawing near to the heart of our affectionate Father. Here, in the light of His glory, there is no twisted vestige of my corruptible past that can long maintain a defiant holdout. It's just a matter of time—everything must change!

A Holy Escort To The Throne

Daniel received a powerful vision in which he saw the Ancient of Days on His throne. Then he saw Jesus approaching His Father's throne. Daniel wrote, "'I was watching in the night visions, and behold, one like the Son of Man, coming with the clouds of heaven! He came to the Ancient of Days, and they brought Him near before Him'" (Daniel 7:13). This verse says "they" brought Jesus near to the throne of heaven.

Who, I want to ask, are "they"? Who *are* these creatures who are escorting Jesus? We're talking about escorting the Second Person of the Trinity, the uncreated Son,
into the very presence of the First Person of the Trinity,
the Ancient of Days. Who qualifies for such an august assignment?

Who, of all God's creatures, has the nobility, the splendor, the dignity, the weightiness, the eminence, the wor-
thiness to serve in such a high and holy role? Whoever
"they" are, they certainly must be big-time dignitaries!
Heavyweights. Serious dudes.

Perhaps they're angels, or cherubim, or seraphim,
or living creatures. Is there another category? I have no
idea.

When I read the words, "They brought Him near before Him," my heart cried out, "Oh Father, give me *that*
kind of an escort into Your presence! Let me be accompa-
nied by angels or cherubim or seraphim as I draw near to
You. I'd like as regal an escort into Your presence as Jesus
Himself has."

Back came the reply, "I'll do that, and one better."

And then I was shown the escort I have into the Father's presence:

> But now in Christ Jesus you who once were
> far off have been brought near by the blood
> of Christ (Ephesians 2:13).

Beloved, we have a more dignified and glorious escort
into the presence of the Ancient of Days than cherubim
or seraphim or living creatures; *we are escorted into God's
presence by the most precious entity in the entire universe—
the blood of Jesus Christ!*

When you approach God with the blood on your life,
you are ushered through the ranks of heaven's hosts, moving past where the angels stand. You come to where the

cherubim are, but still you keep moving forward. You come to the seraphim, but your place is closer still. You come to where the living creatures live in the throne of God, and you step beyond even their proximity to the throne. The blood brings you nearer than any of heaven's hosts, right into the embrace of the Father Himself.

Sprinkled Every Day

Since we have such a glorious entrance into the presence of God, we should take advantage of the sprinkling of blood more often. In fact, I'm recommending we make it a daily practice.

I realize that I'm suggesting something that has not been consistently practiced by 99% of believers. I reckon that most people reading this book fully agree that receiving the sprinkled blood of Christ is a powerful means of cleansing one's conscience. My hunch, though, is that most Christians rarely do it. We give mental adherence theologically to its efficacy, but in terms of actual practice, most of us almost never invoke the sprinkled blood over our lives.

YOU HAVE A MORE DIGNIFIED AND GLORIOUS ESCORT INTO THE PRESENCE OF THE ANCIENT OF DAYS THAN CHERUBIM OR SERAPHIM OR LIVING CREATURES.

It might be tempting to think, "I've been doing okay without it. My pastor has never mentioned it. My friends don't practice it. I don't know anybody who gets sprinkled every day. If it's so important, why isn't anybody doing it?" I'm not meaning to sound challenging or accusatory; rather, I'm wanting to entice you with an invitation to something glorious.

Is it possible that God has something greater for you which you haven't fully tasted yet?

The frequency with which we get sprinkled with blood might find its similitude in the Lord's Table. The question is often asked, "How often should one receive Communion." When Jesus said "as often as" (quoted by Paul in 1 Corinthians 11:25), His inference seemed to be, "as often as you might desire." You can do it monthly, weekly, daily, or even more than once a day if you like. There are no rules that say, "You've had Communion today; you can't have it again until tomorrow."

Sprinkling with blood operates in a similar way. You can receive sprinkling as often as you desire.

JESUS DIED TO BRING ME INTO THE THRONE-ROOM; WHY, THEN, SHOULD I NEGLECT SUCH AN AWESOME PRIVILEGE?

Getting sprinkled with blood has become an integral part of my morning, and has empowered my intimacy with God in a delightful way. I've latched onto something—the wisdom of daily sprinkling—and I want to sell the world on it.

When I really understood what the sprinkling of Christ's blood provides for me, that's when I decided I wanted to get sprinkled every day. Through His blood I enter into the Holiest, draw up into the bosom of the Father, and blaze with holy passions in the presence of His glory. Jesus killed Himself—as it were—to bring me into the throneroom; why, then, should I neglect the greatest privilege a human can enjoy?

God forbid that I should lightly esteem the very reason for which Jesus hung on the cross. My heart is steadfast; I will get sprinkled with blood every day and draw near to God with boldness. This is my glorious privilege, to live every day of my life in the bosom of the Father. This is where I can *live;* and by His grace, this is where I will *die.*

Chapter 5

SEATED BETWEEN FATHER *and* SON

I get sprinkled with blood every morning. And when I do, I see myself instantly in the throneroom, standing before God with full acceptance, confident in His love, and enjoying intimate fellowship with Him.

And now I want to explain what I see happening next.

Getting My Bearings At The Throne

Look with me at the last verse of Psalm 109—"For He shall stand at the right hand of the poor, to save him from those who condemn him" (Psalm 109:31). Since I am among "the poor" in spirit, this verse indicates that Jesus is standing at my right hand.

Let's compare that truth with the next verse in your Bible—a comparison that doesn't happen readily because of the chapter break. The next verse goes on to say, "The LORD said to my Lord, 'Sit at My right hand, till I make Your enemies Your footstool'" (Psalm 110:1).

Thus, the first verse of Psalm 110 has Jesus at the right hand of the Father.

Now, look at it again:

❖ The last verse of Psalm 109 has Jesus at *my* right hand.[1]

❖ The first verse of Psalm 110 has Jesus at the *Father's* right hand.

So Jesus is at the right hand of both the Father and me. Hmm. How does this work?

As I was contemplating the throneroom geography described by these verses, the most reasonable conclusion that began to emerge was this: The Father must be on my *left* hand.

Here's what I then began to visualize (with the eye of faith). I saw Jesus on my right hand, and the Father on my left. This arrangement seemed consistent to me with Psalm 110, because it still places Jesus at the Father's right hand.

ON MY LEFT IS THE FATHER. ON MY RIGHT IS JESUS. AND IN THE MIDDLE IS—ME.

On my left is the Father. On my right is Jesus. And in the middle is—me. Or in your case—you.

A Childhood Illustration

When I was a kid, I remember my parents would sometimes embrace in the kitchen, expressing their

---

1 Some have wondered why I see Jesus in Psalm 109:31 when the Hebrew word used there is YAHWEH. I have two primary reasons. First, YAHWEH is often used in the Old Testament as a name for Christ in His pre-incarnate state. Just a couple examples would be Genesis 18:1 and Exodus 3:7, but there are many others. And second, whenever YAHWEH is described as "standing" in the Old Testament, in my observation it is almost always a reference to Christ. A couple examples would be Zechariah 3:1-2 and Joshua 5:13-6:2. Whenever the Father is clearly meant by YAHWEH, and a bodily position is ascribed to Him, according to my research He is always said to be seated (1Kings 22:19 and others).

tenderness for each other. Whenever I saw that affection happening, I would always rush over and immediately wiggle my way between them until I was smack in the middle. I, too, wanted in on the love-exchange. I figured, if we're going to be doing the lovey-dovey thing right now, I want in on the action!

The only problem was, I kept growing. The bigger I got, the less enthusiastic my parents became with this arrangement. Having 110 pounds jammed like a wad of wiggling blubber between them during a tender body embrace did not seem to meet, for some reason, their standards of "romantic." Eventually, my dad took me aside and said, "You know, Bobby, sometimes I want to embrace your mother without you getting in the middle between us." His protest fell on deaf ears. Because as far as I was concerned, if there's affection happening, then sign me up.

Between Father And Son

I'm 50 years old now and nothing's changed. I get sprinkled with the blood of Jesus, barge with boldness into the throneroom—"It's me again!"—and gaze upon Holiness. And when I look at the throne, I see *affection!* For there, seated together on the throne, are the Father and Son in an everlasting love-lock of abandoned affection and fiery loyalty.

When I see this kind of affection, I want in. So I just worm my way between the Father and Son (bold with confidence because of the blood) until I'm smack dab in the middle. Then, I turn around and sit down with Christ in heavenly places (Ephesians 2:6). The Father on my left. Jesus on my right. Me in the middle.

And that's where I like to spend my day: In the bosom of the Father (John 1:18) and leaning on the breast of Jesus (John 13:23). I envision myself snuggled in the middle of the Father/Son love-embrace and lapping up all the affection.

Come there with me. See yourself approaching God with confidence because of the sprinkled blood. Now, interject yourself between the Father and Son, and be seated with Christ in heavenly places. Turn to the Father on your left and express your love. Turn to the Son on your right and worship Him. Enjoy this place of being nestled between the Father and the Son. This is the nearness Jesus destined for you when He offered His blood on your behalf.

Now that I'm here, right between God and Jesus, here's how I like to see the thing: If the Father wants to say anything to the Son, He's going to have to go through me. And if the Son wants to say anything to the Father, He's going to have to go through me. In my noblest imaginations, I envision the Father and Son of necessity including me in their intimate dialogue because I have been joined to them—one in heart, purpose, and affection.

A Hypothetical Father/Son Conversation

And here's how I imagine the conversation sounding.

Father (speaking to the Son, through me):

"Son, You are the greatest delight of My heart because You laid Your life down for me." (And as that word passes through my spirit, my heart responds, "Yes, Abba, I lay my life down for You.")

Son (speaking to the Father, through me):

"Yes, Abba. Of *course* I laid My life down for You. You *asked* Me to."

Father (to the Son, again through me):

"But Son, I gave you such a bitter cup to drink. And You drank it to the very dregs. You loved Me in the place of ultimate suffering. You have moved My heart at the deepest level. How can I adequately express the fierceness of My loyalty to You?"

Son (replying to the Father, through me):

"Abba, if You gave Me another cup, I'd drink it again. Because I adore You and I'm absolutely loyal to You. I'll do anything for You." (As that word moves through me, my heart resonates with it, "Yes, Abba, I also will do anything for You, I am Yours.")

Father:

"Son, do You realize how deeply Your fidelity moves My heart? I offered a bitter cup to Lucifer as well, but he looked at the cup, became offended, accused Me of being a tyrant, and turned a third of heaven's angels against Me. My intention was to bring him to greater honor, but He couldn't see it. He said My leadership style was oppressive, that I was a tyrannical Father—he called it cosmic child abuse—and he got a third of heaven to agree with him. But You didn't partner with Lucifer's accusation. When I gave You a bitter cup, You drank it to the bottom. Son, Your loyalty to Me in the most difficult of times was unwavering, and I'll never forget it. My love is Yours—forever."

> IF THE FATHER WANTS TO SAY ANYTHING TO THE SON, HE'S GOING TO HAVE TO GO THROUGH ME.

Son:

"But Abba, when I was in the lowest place, when I had descended to My lowest hell, when the caverns of Hades echoed with shrieks of triumph at My descension, when the sorrows of Sheol were wrapped around My brain like seaweed, You reached down into My darkness and lifted Me out of My pit"—(and as these words pass through my spirit on their way to the Father my heart resounds, "Yes, Abba, You will lift me out of my pit, too")—"and You have

exalted Me to the highest place and have seated Me with
Yourself, again, on Your throne. O Abba, I love You with
everything within Me!"

Father:

"Son, if You think I have finished exalting You, You
can think again. Because I haven't hardly even *begun*
Your exaltation. Right now, the world over, Your name
is mocked, profaned, and blasphemed. You are viewed
by many across the earth as boring and irrelevant. Some
think you're a myth—they don't even believe You exist.
But it's not going to end like that. Just sit here at My right
hand, Son, and watch while I finish Your story. By the
time I'm finished with this planet, every knee will bow (of
those in heaven, and of those on the earth, and of those
under the earth) and every tongue will confess that You
are Lord."

Jesus Is Still Waiting

Jesus' exaltation is not yet complete, but the Day is
just around the corner when the Father will fulfill all His promises to
His Son. In the meantime, He waits.

IF YOU'RE WAITING
ON GOD, YOU'RE IN
GOOD COMPANY;
JESUS IS ALSO
WAITING ON GOD.

How about you? Are you waiting on God? Has God made promises to you which have not yet been
realized in your life? If so, you're not
the only one. Jesus Christ is also living with unfulfilled
promises. The Father has promised the earth and its fullness to Him, but it has not all yet been brought into sub-
jection to Him.

But be assured of this: Not one word of all God's good
promise to His Son will fail. Every promise shall be fulfilled! Jesus shall reign over planet Earth, and the hearts
of His people shall be fully His possession. It *will* happen.

Nothing can stop it, for the Father is determined to fulfill His word to His Son.

In the same way, you can be assured of this: Every promise God has given you shall be fulfilled. He is good to His word; what He promises He performs.

If you're waiting on God, you're in good company; Jesus is also waiting on God.

The Holy Spirit

I was telling how I get sprinkled with blood, then see myself seated with Christ in heavenly places. Let's come back to that. Sandwiched between Father and Son, I find myself the exhilarated recipient of the affections that flow between them. The Father and Son express their love for each other in a way that tells me I am loved with the same fiery passions.

Here's the next thing I visualize.

From my position on the throne where I'm seated with Christ in heavenly places, I look out upon the heavenly panorama before me, and the first thing I see is the Holy Spirit. He stands before me in the same way John saw Him in Revelation 4:5. I see seven lamps of fire, which are the seven Spirits of God that burn before the throne. Now that I'm seated on the throne, the seven-fold Spirit of God is directly facing me.

I pray a simple prayer, "Holy Spirit, come into me." I invite Him, with all seven of His fiery Spirits (whatever that means!), to enter my belly and ignite my body, soul, mind, heart—my entire being—with every living flame that ignites His heart.

I receive His very fire into my bosom. Scripture asks, "Can a man take fire to his bosom, and his clothes not be burned?" (Proverbs 6:27). I sure hope not! My hope is that as I absorb the living fires of the Holy Spirit into my bosom, all the filthy garments of my old manner of life are burned away and everything is made new.

So here we rest. On our left we're in the bosom of the Father, feasting on His affections; to our right we're leaning on the breast of Jesus, drawing upon His grace. And straight before us, the Holy Spirit is entering and igniting us with the fellowship of His eternal fires. We're enveloped in the affections of the Godhead—all because of the blood of Jesus. Tell me: If this is where we reside, how can we lose? How can we possibly fail? No matter what conflict or trial we may encounter, we are on an inexorable path to overcoming victory. When we live in the shadow of the Almighty, we're unstoppable.

"If God is for us, who can be against us?" (Romans 8:31).

Chapter 6

DRAWING NEAR *to* GOD

The kind of intimacy we've been talking about is the very thing that God has always wanted with His people. God is extremely relational, and He created us in His image so that we might long for Him in the way He longs for us. From the very beginning, God has always wanted communing friendship with man. We see that in the way He came every day to visit with Adam and Eve in the Garden of Eden (Genesis 3:8).

The Bible launches with a God who is seeking fellowship with man, and it ends with the same motif. The book of Revelation details how God has determined this present age will end. We might have thought that God was preparing us for heaven, but in an unexpected twist, the saga of redemptive history ends with God leaving heaven and coming to earth to be with man.

> Now I saw a new heaven and a new earth, for the first heaven and the first earth had passed away. Also there was no more sea. Then I, John, saw the holy city, New Jerusalem, coming down out of heaven from God, prepared as a bride adorned for her husband. And I heard a loud voice from heaven saying, "Behold, the tabernacle of God is with men,

and He will dwell with them, and they shall
be His people. God Himself will be with them
and be their God" (Revelation 21:1-3).

First, John sees the bride of Christ—the New Jerusalem—leaving God in heaven and descending to earth in
order to be married to the Bridegroom here on the earth.
Then, in the next verse, John hears a declaration of what
is to follow: *God Himself* will leave heaven and descend to
earth! It's almost too stunning to comprehend.

The Father has not designed a way to move man from
earth to heaven; rather, He has designed a way for Him to
move from heaven to earth. The story ends with heaven
on earth. God's longing to be near mankind is so acute
that He is planning to pick up and relocate His entire
home base—all for the purpose of being close to us!

THE FATHER HAS NOT DESIGNED A WAY TO MOVE MAN FROM EARTH TO HEAVEN; RATHER, HE HAS DESIGNED A WAY FOR HIM TO MOVE FROM HEAVEN TO EARTH.

Right now, we are laboring with
the Holy Spirit to prepare our planet
for the coming of Christ. Once He
comes, we will then labor with Him
during "the millennium" to prepare
the planet for the coming of the Father. That's one reason why that period will be 1,000 years in duration
(see Revelation 20)—it will take that
long to get the planet ready for the
Father's coming. Why is He coming? He wants to be near
us.

Attempts At Intimacy

*The Old Testament is the winding saga of God's attempts
to get close to His people.* First, He had to produce in them
a desire to call upon Him. He did that by putting them
in Egypt and placing them in slavery. Their oppressors
made them so miserable that they cried out to God for

intervention. In response to Israel's cries, God visited them in Egypt, released them from slavery, and set up camp in their midst. He drew near to them because He wanted relationship.

But there was a problem. There was a fundamental mismatch between God's holiness and the people's sins. Because of His holiness, God could not tolerate the people's sinfulness. As a result, people died. The wilderness became strewn with a long trail of corpses. God's chosen people were dying because God had entered the camp. Eventually the people complained to Moses, "'Whoever even comes near the tabernacle of the LORD must die. Shall we all utterly die?'" (Numbers 17:13). God acknowledged this problem when He said, "'I will not go up in your midst, lest I consume you on the way, for you are a stiff-necked people'" (Exodus 33:3).

It was a massive quandary. Out of His longing for intimacy God had come near the people, but as a result thousands were dying. A solution had to be found.

God's solution was this: the sprinkling of blood. Blood would have to be shed and sprinkled. If blood were shed properly, it would atone for (cover) the people's sins, and God would be able to reside in their midst without killing them. This is what God meant when He said, "'And you shall attend to the duties of the sanctuary and the duties of the altar, that there may be no more wrath on the children of Israel'" (Numbers 18:5).

The entire sacrificial system of the Old Testament was designed to pacify God's wrath as He came to dwell among His people.

God was basically saying, "I am coming to dwell with you. But if I become angry with you because of your sinfulness, it will bode ill for you. I am providing, therefore, a way for you to allay My wrath. If you will honor My three feasts and My sacrificial system, My wrath will be satisfied and you will be blessed by My proximity. If you neglect these sacrifices, however, My nearness will actually be to your detriment."

For God and man to live together, it was essential that animal sacrifices be established. But they could not happen in Egypt because the Egyptians would not allow them. The Egyptians despised the Israelites' animal sacrifices and categorically forbad them (Exodus 8:26). In order to inaugurate the sprinkling of blood, God had to get the Israelites out of Egypt.

Blood was not shed so that God could come down and draw near to His people; God had *already* come down and visited His people. Blood was shed so that the people could *survive* His presence.

The whole sacrificial system was actually for God, not man. It enabled God to do what was in His heart—to draw near to His people—without having to judge (hurt) them. God's desire has always been that we be enriched from intimacy with Him, not punished (judged) because of it. That's why God instituted the shedding of innocent blood. The animal sacrifices provided a way for God to come to earth and be close to man. If God was to dwell with man, sin would have to be judged. Instead of people having to die, innocent animals died in their place. In this way, the animal sacrifices pointed to the ultimate sacrifice, the innocent Lamb of God, who would die for the sins of the whole world.

So again, the shedding of blood was for the purpose of intimacy.

Sprinkling With Blood In The Old Testament

The New Testament blessing of sprinkling with blood derives from its Old Testament precedent. Here's the Old Testament background.

The animal sacrifices provided for intimacy with God, but at four levels of significance. The people could draw near at one level, the Levites at a closer level, the priests drew closer still, and the high priest came near at the greatest level of intimacy.

(a) The people. The shed blood of the animal sacrifices made atonement for the sins of the people so that they could "come near the sanctuary" (Numbers 8:19). The closest the people could get, in that old dispensation, was to stand outside the sanctuary.

(b) The Levites. The blood enabled the Levites (sons of Levi, one of the Israelite tribes) to draw closer to God than those of the other tribes of Israel. They were able to enter the sanctuary itself. They could stand in the outer court of the temple where they served the priests and ministered to the Lord (Deuteronomy 10:8). Thus, God brought the Levites "'near to Himself, to do the work of the tabernacle of the LORD, and to stand before the congregation to serve them'" (Numbers 16:9). They served the needs of the priests and of the tabernacle (Numbers 18:3). If they performed their ministry properly, there would be "'no plague among the children of Israel when the children of Israel come near the sanctuary'" (Numbers 8:19).

> BLOOD WAS NOT SHED SO THAT GOD COULD COME DOWN AND DRAW NEAR TO HIS PEOPLE; BLOOD WAS SHED SO THAT THE PEOPLE COULD *SURVIVE* HIS PRESENCE.

(c) The priests. The blood enabled the priests (the descendants of Aaron) to draw even closer to God than the Levites. They commonly entered the Holy Place and were able to handle all the articles of the sanctuary (Numbers 18:3). They were also able to offer incense on the golden altar of incense (1 Chronicles 6:49). There was one priest, however, who could draw even nearer to God. He was called the high priest.

(d) The high priest.

The blood enabled the high priest to draw closer to God than any of the other priests. This special privilege took place just one day each year, on the Day of Atonement, when the high priest was commanded to enter the Holy of Holies. (The Holy of Holies was the innermost chamber of the sanctuary which contained the ark of the covenant and the mercy seat.) It was on this day that the sprinkling of blood found its most meaningful expression.

On that very high and holy day, the high priest would first of all enter the Holy of Holies with a censer of hot coals and hands loaded with incense. Once inside, he would place the incense on the hot coals and then set the censer down so that the smoke would cover the mercy seat. He then went out, took some of the blood of the bull that had been sacrificed, re-entered the Holy of Holies (that was now filled with smoke) and sprinkled the blood of the bull to atone for his own sins. One-two-three-four-five-six-seven-eight. Eight times the blood was sprinkled upon and before the mercy seat. Then he went out, offered the goat as an offering, and brought the blood of the goat into the Holy of Holies to expiate for the sins of the entire nation. One-two-three-four-five-six-seven-eight. Eight times the blood of the goat was sprinkled upon the mercy seat in the same manner as the bull's blood. He alone could minister this close to God, right there at the ark of the covenant, in the very place where God dwelled. Then he took the censer in hand and exited the Holy of Holies, not to return for another year.

Thus, the sprinkling of blood made it possible for God

to dwell among and fellowship with His people. Every time we get sprinkled with blood and draw near to God, we are essentially re-enacting what the high priest did on the Day of Atonement, for once again we enter the Holy of Holies to minister to the Lord.

Our Covenant Is So Much Greater!

Under the Old Covenant, only one man (the high priest) could draw near to the very presence of God, and even so, he could do so only once a year (Hebrews 9:7). Furthermore, when he drew near to God on that one special day, he did it *quickly*. He hastened to perform his required service of incense and sprinkling, and then he got out of the Holy of Holies as fast as he could.

If I had the chance, I would have said to Aaron (the high priest), "Aaron! You have the greatest privilege in the entire nation! You get to enter the inner chamber where God Himself resides. You alone have the privilege of gazing upon the glory of God who dwells between the cherubim.[1] Aaron, *take your time*. Enjoy the moment. Relish your unique privilege. Slow down, and gaze with long, loving fascination at the wonder of God's glory. Inhale, breathe it in. Go slow. *Enjoy!*"

I imagine Aaron's retort, "Are you kidding? When I'm

---

1 The Holy of Holies had no window nor source of light in it; it was shrouded in complete darkness. So when the high priest entered on the Day of Atonement, he would have stepped into a black room. There are some who believe, however, that God manifested Himself on the Day of Atonement in the form of a light between the wings of the cherubim. This would have given the high priest enough light to perform his service, and it would have also allowed him to peer into the glory of God. This theory is based largely upon Jonathan's Targum rendering of Leviticus 16:2, which reads, "'for in my cloud the glory of my Shechinah, or divine Majesty, shall be revealed upon the mercy seat.'" The NKJV renders it, "'For I will appear in the cloud above the mercy seat.'"

standing before the ark of the covenant, I'm scared out of my wits. One wrong move and I'm dead![2] Go slow? Not me. I'm getting out of there as fast as I can!"

It was one man, once a year, fast.

Thank God for the blood of Jesus! Because of Christ's shed blood, now it's not only one man who can draw near to the very presence of God; now, *all of us* can draw near! And it's not limited to one day a year; we can draw near to God 24/7/365 (any time of day, any day of the year). And we don't have to hurry; we can enter into the immediate presence of God through the sprinkled blood of Christ and *stay there*!

How Near Is Near?

While the sprinkled blood on the mercy seat allowed the people to draw somewhat near to God, nonetheless they were tentative about their approach. We see this same uncertainty when, just after their exodus from Egypt, the Israelites came to Mt. Sinai and prepared to draw close to God.

BECAUSE OF CHRIST'S SHED BLOOD, NOW IT'S NOT ONLY ONE MAN WHO CAN DRAW NEAR TO THE VERY PRESENCE OF GOD; NOW, ALL OF US CAN DRAW NEAR!

God was going to come down onto Mt. Sinai and manifest Himself to the entire nation of Israel. He was getting ready to speak to them audibly with a thunderous, terrifying voice. Once God would descend on the mountain, that would make the mountain holy. The encounter carried inherent dangers, because if someone made a wrong move they could be killed for

---

2   In Leviticus 16:13, God said in so many words, "Aaron needs to offer the incense properly when he enters the Holiest on the Day of Atonement, or he's dead." High priests always performed their ministry on the Day of Atonement under fear of death.

it. God came to Moses, therefore, with some very specific instructions. He wanted His people to survive the encounter. Here's an excerpt from God's instructions.

> "And let them be ready for the third day. For on the third day the LORD will come down upon Mount Sinai in the sight of all the people. You shall set bounds for the people all around, saying, *'Take heed to yourselves that you do not go up to the mountain or touch its base. Whoever touches the mountain shall surely be put to death.* Not a hand shall touch him, but he shall surely be stoned or shot with an arrow; whether man or beast, he shall not live.' When the trumpet sounds long, *they shall come near the mountain*" (Exodus 19:11-13).

God's warning was very clear: Take heed; don't come too close, or you'll be put to death.

But that ominous warning was then followed by this mysterious command: "They shall come near the mountain." After being warned about getting *too* close, they are then commanded to draw near.

"How near is near?" I can imagine some sincere soul inquiring.

It was quite the predicament. Hang back too far and you're in rebellion; get too close and you're dead. Little wonder the people drew near timidly and tentatively! They had to draw near without getting too near.

"How near is near?"

Thank God for the blood of Jesus Christ! Because of Christ's shed blood, we can now enter with *boldness* into the very throneroom of heaven. No more timidity. No more hesitation. The blood has given us confidence. We know we're accepted into the eager embrace of our affectionate heavenly Father.

Gone forever is any line of demarcation that says, "You

GONE FOREVER IS ANY LINE OF DEMARCATION THAT SAYS, "YOU CAN GO SO FAR BUT NO FURTHER."

can go so far but no further." All the limitations have been rescinded, and we're playing by a totally new set of rules. Now the compelling question is, "How close can you get?"

The old question: "How do I know when I've come too close?"

The new question: "How near are you willing to draw?"

Draw Near To God!

To endure the cross, Jesus had to understand what His work would accomplish. He had to understand *purpose*. He had to have ownership of the intended end. What was that purpose?

> Jesus, what did You see when You hung on the cross? During Your suffering, when You pictured us in the bosom of the Father, what implications scrolled before Your eyes? What was so powerful about this intimacy that it kept you on the cross until Your last dying breath? Surely You wouldn't die for anything less than the absolute transformation of our world. Will You help us see what You saw? Would you reveal the implications of an intimacy so revolutionizing that You were willing to endure the Father's wrath in order to procure it for us?

Here's how Jesus chose to change human history. He purposed within Himself, "I'll die on Calvary; then I'll sprinkle them with My blood; that will bring them into intimacy with the Father; if they'll draw near to God, they will change their world." Jesus died, beloved, to get you into the Father's bosom. It's that important.

Oh, that I were more skillful at crafting words to adequately express the desirability of drawing near to God! Christ's sacrifice means that the thing that once produced death in us (proximity to God) now gives us life. And that which once nourished us (sin) is now poisonous to us. His sacrifice has produced within us a complete transformation of our genetic code.

Now I run into that from which I once fled (intimacy with God). And I flee from that into which I once rushed (sin). My compatibility system has been radically inverted. O glorious transformation! I'm a new man in Christ—because of the blood of His cross.

"Draw near to God," James beckons, "and He will draw near to you" (4:8). Take a step toward God, and He takes a step toward you. Take another, and so does He. For every movement you make into the heart of God, He reciprocates by moving closer into your heart.

James 4:8 leads logically to this conclusion: You can draw still closer to God. In other words, you have not yet reached the fullness of the intimacy Jesus died to provide. There's more. There's more. There's more. Pursue it! Draw closer still!

CHRIST'S SACRIFICE MEANS THAT THE THING THAT ONCE PRODUCED DEATH IN US (PROXIMITY TO GOD) NOW GIVES US LIFE.

If you're in a swirl of spiritual warfare right now, and not quite sure how to take on your enemy or how to move forward, let me tell you what to do. Get sprinkled with Christ's blood, come into the throneroom, and stay there. *The most militant thing you can do is draw near to God.*

When you're near to God, the Bible says you can call upon Him for "whatever reason" (Deuteronomy 4:7). In other words, you can ask Him for *anything you want*. This is the privilege of intimacy. Jesus Himself affirmed you can ask for anything when He said, "'If you abide in Me, and My words abide in you, you will ask *what you desire*, and it shall be done for you'" (John 15:7). Jesus further added, "'And *whatever you ask* in My name, that I will do, that the Father may be glorified in the Son'" (John 14:13).

Ask Him for the world. He already promised it to you. The world is yours, it's part of your Abrahamic covenant (Romans 4:13-16). "Abba, now that I'm joined to Your heart because of Christ's sprinkled blood, I want to ask You for the innermost desire of my heart. I'm asking that You give the world to Your Son. Give Him the affections of every human being on this planet. Turn the hearts of every nation toward Your beloved Son, until every knee bows and every tongue confesses that Jesus is Lord. Give Him the world. Give us the world. Make it ours!"

You Can't Go Wrong By Drawing Near

If you're ever unsure about your status with God—that is, if you've been in a season of compromise and you're not sure what He's thinking about the choices you've been making—the smartest thing you can do is draw near. You'll get along better with God by drawing near than by hanging back.

Several Bible stories illustrate this truth. I'll mention just two. On one occasion, Judah was wanting to make a special appeal to the stern Egyptian master who was before him. Judah didn't know the Egyptian master was actually Joseph, his brother; all he knew was that the man had total authority over his life and he had to be placated. So what did Judah do?

> Then Judah *came near to him* and said: "O my lord, please let your servant speak a word in my lord's hearing, and do not let your anger

burn against your servant; for you are even like Pharaoh" (Genesis 44:18).

By drawing near to Joseph, Judah was demonstrating honor, respect, fear, a regard for protocol, and a recognition of the superior office of the Egyptian master. When he drew near and made his appeal in humility, Judah won the heart of his brother.

The same thing happens in our relationship with God. When we draw near to Him in humility, He turns His favor toward us. To reinforce this point, let me mention one more story.

The book of Esther contains the story of two queens who broke the law. While both Vashti and Esther broke the law of Persia, the way they did it made all the difference in their respective destinies. Vashti broke the law by spurning the king's summons when he had requested her presence (Esther 1:12); Esther broke the law by drawing near to the king at a time when her presence was unsolicited (Esther 4:11; 5:1-2).

Vashti broke the law by staying away; Esther broke the law by drawing near.

The king became furious with Vashti! It wasn't simply that she broke the law; it was that she broke the law by withholding herself. When Esther broke the law, the king's response was totally different. He lifted his scepter and welcomed her into his throneroom. Why? Because even though she was breaking the law, she was doing it by drawing near.

> WHEN WE DRAW NEAR TO HIM IN HUMILITY, HE TURNS HIS FAVOR TOWARD US.

"But I can't draw near to God in my present condition," someone might object. "If I were to draw near to God right now, I think He'd fry me."

That's what the accuser wants you to believe—because he wants to keep you separated from God. But the truth is exactly the opposite. *If you draw near to God with a sincere heart, you will never incur His wrath.* You incur His wrath by staying away. Draw near in sincerity and truth and you will invoke His favor. The Father yearns for this kind of nearness with you.

"But isn't it fearful to get this close to God?" someone else might counter. "I'm afraid of getting close to God in my current condition." The truth is, the fear of the Lord catapults us into the face of Christ. If what you're feeling is causing you to draw back, it's not the true fear of the Lord. The fear of the Lord, properly taught, always presses us toward God because we realize that near is the only safe place to be.

Even Satan Understands the Power of Intimacy

The accuser will do his utmost to keep you distant from God, a reality that is illustrated in the life of Joshua, the high priest during Zechariah's day.

The book of Zechariah was written at a time when Israel was experiencing a spiritual revival. The temple in Jerusalem was being restored, along with all the Old Testament feasts. Israel had been without a high priest for many years, but now a man named Joshua was being properly installed and ordained to this ministry.

YOU INCUR HIS WRATH BY STAYING AWAY.

At his installation, however, Satan himself stood up to oppose this appointment (Zechariah 3:1). Satan didn't want Joshua ministering as a priest before God. Why would Satan stand up to resist a man as weak as Joshua? (When you look at his life, you realize that Joshua was a spiritually weak man.) The reason seems to be that Satan knew if

Joshua were fully ordained as high priest, it would mean that once again a man would approach the immediate presence of God in the Holiest. Satan understood the power of intimacy and realized his kingdom was at risk if Joshua were to become high priest. He tried to portray Joshua as disqualified from drawing near to God. Thankfully, Satan's attempt to disqualify Joshua from serving as high priest was unsuccessful.

Now, a man (Joshua) would be stepping into the very throneroom of God once a year. And from that intimacy grace would flow to the entire community of God's redeemed people.

Little wonder Satan tried to stop Joshua's ordination. When Joshua came into intimacy with God, it provided a platform with powerful potential for kingdom blessing. *When God is in intimacy with man, and God and man are moving forward together, the world can be turned upside-down.*

We Don't Naturally Tend To Draw Near

Drawing near to God, although it's the wisest thing a human can do, is not the normal tendency of human nature. Some of us need help to "stumble onto" this wisdom. Left to ourselves, we will not pursue intimacy with radical Kingdom violence. So sometimes God will hijack our trajectory. What initially appears to be a disruption is eventually seen to be an invitation to draw near. Sometimes God is kind enough to not leave us to ourselves.

David was a man accosted of God, so he was able to say with understanding, "Blessed is the man You choose, and cause to approach You, that he may dwell in Your courts" (Psalm 65:4). God has many ways of "causing" us to approach Him. Often God ends up having to use painful circumstances to motivate us toward Him. *Do not despise the means God uses to bring you into intimacy.*

Perhaps He is loving you enough to save you from the perverseness of your own ways.

In a single verse, Zephaniah gave four reasons why God would allow uncomfortable restriction in the life of His beloved: to cultivate obedience to His voice; to trigger profound character transformation; to produce mountain-moving faith; and to foster a lifestyle of intimacy with God (see Zephaniah 3:2). Drawing near to God may not be our natural proclivity, but God will chasten us in order to bring us into the intimacy for which we long.

When we pull away from God, we're actually acting like a beast. That's what we see in Psalm 32:9, "Do not be like the horse or like the mule, which have no understanding, which must be harnessed with bit and bridle, else they will not come near you" (Psalm 32:9). It's not in the nature of beasts to draw near. There's something beastly in the heart of man that causes him to wander away from his source of life. Can you hear the Lord imploring us to be wise and understanding instead of mulish? We're interested in conquering the next mountain; but God's interested in intimacy. When will we learn to draw near?

DO NOT DESPISE THE MEANS GOD USES TO BRING YOU INTO INTIMACY.

Drawing Near For Judgment

I want to close this chapter by pointing to one of the more fascinating and mysterious principles in the Bible related to nearness with God. I'm using the word "mysterious" in its biblical sense. A mystery, in the Bible, is a spiritual truth that has more depth to it than is readily evident at first glance. It invites deeper study. A biblical mystery whispers, "There's gold to be found in this truth, but you'll have to go digging to find it."

Here's the verse I want us to consider.

"Keep silence before Me, O coastlands, and
let the people renew their strength! Let them
come near, then let them speak; let us come
near together for judgment" (Isaiah 41:1).

I invite you to pause for a moment, pick up your Bible,
and peruse the last five verses of Isaiah 40. Those verses
provide the context for the verse above. God's people were
complaining, "God has overlooked us. We have stood on
His word, claimed His promises, and prayed to Him un-
ceasingly; but He is not noticing or responding."

In the face of that accusation, God's first response is,
"'Keep silence before Me, O coastlands'" (Isaiah 41:1a).
In other words, He is saying to the
ends of the earth, "Be quiet! I've
heard enough of your accusations.
The world over, men are accusing
Me of being unresponsive to their
prayers. But the smartest thing
you could do right now would be
to stop accusing Me, and just shut
your mouth! I happen to be working with far more infor-
mation and understanding than you could ever process or
appreciate. So be silent!"

WE DRAW NEAR TO
MAKE JOINT DECISIONS
THAT DETERMINE
THE DESTINY OF OUR
PLANET.

God's second piece of advice: "'Let the people renew
their strength!'" (Isaiah 41:1b). Or, to use the language
of Isaiah 40:31, "Get off your pinwheel, calm yourself,
and wait on Me. Your own efforts have wearied you. If
you would wait on Me instead of running in circles, you
would regain your strength and rise up on the wings of
renewed perspective."

God's third piece of counsel: "'Let them come
near, then let them speak'" (Isaiah 41:1c). In other
words, "You're assailing Me with your many words,

and you're doing it from a distance. When you grill Me with your questions from afar, they hit Me like accusations. Accusations never unlock My blessings. Why don't you change your approach? Start by shutting up. Then draw near to Me. Enter into fiery communion with My generous heart. Once intimacy has been firmly established between us, then you could speak whatever is on your mind and it would come to Me as a lovesick prayer rather than a hurled accusation."

Look now, at God's fourth—and most fascinating— invitation: "'Let us come near together for judgment'" (Isaiah 41:1d). Intimacy with God culminates in a partnership in which we actually enter into the processes of judgment with Him. The invitation infers, "If you would draw near to Me, we would begin to enter into the dialogue of intimacy. I would hear your heart; you would hear My heart; and we would arrive at the right judgment (decision) together."

God is saying the purpose of intimacy is that we might participate with Him in making joint decisions that determine the destiny of our planet.

Selah

Chapter 7

HOLINESS: PROXIMITY *to the* THRONE

When speaking of the blood of Christ, we must also speak of holiness, for Scripture brings the two together. The leading text for this book conjoins the two when it declares that the blood of Christ qualifies us to enter with boldness into "the Holiest." The Holiest is the very Holy of Holies in heaven where God dwells. Think of it—there is no holier place in all of heaven than where we live!

> Therefore, brethren, having boldness to enter the Holiest by the blood of Jesus, by a new and living way which He consecrated for us, through the veil, that is, His flesh, and having a High Priest over the house of God, let us draw near with a true heart in full assurance of faith, having our hearts sprinkled from an evil conscience and our bodies washed with pure water (Hebrews 10:19-22).

The term "the Holiest" assumes that there are degrees of holiness. Degrees of holiness vary according to proximity to the throne. Holier places are those places nearer to the throne. The Holiest is the very bosom of God Himself. Since we have access to the Holiest, it's impossible to find a place in God's highest heaven that is holier than the place where we now reside. Hebrews 10 says we get sprinkled with blood that we might enter into holiness. A couple chapters later, Hebrews goes on to say it's God's intention that we be "partakers of His holiness" (Hebrews 12:10). To share in God's holiness is the ultimate honor any human could enjoy, and the sprinkled blood of Christ upon our lives makes it possible.

Holiness is a *place*. We have sometimes conceived of holiness as a behavioral code of dos and don'ts, but holiness is not as much something we do as it is a place we enter. "The Holiest" is a place. It's a spiritual place in heavenly realms that we enter by faith through the sprinkled blood of Christ. It's the innermost chamber of the temple in heaven, the place where God Himself resides. Christ's blood is our "All Access Pass" to the most private living room of the An-

HOLINESS IS A PLACE.

cient of Days. This blood authorizes us to step into the command center of the universe, to tremble with affection in the presence of His glorious power, and *stay there*.

When you are here, in the inner chambers of the King, you are a partaker of His holiness. Why? Because holiness is a place. Let me substantiate that even further.

Holy Ground

When Moses saw the bush that burned but wasn't consumed, he approached it to get a better look. As he drew near, he stepped unwittingly onto holy ground. Why was the ground holy? Because God was present in that place, and God's presence made that place holy.

If you were to find that same plot of ground on Mt. Sinai, it would not be holy today. God would not command you to take your shoes off, like He commanded Moses, because that ground is no longer holy. It was holy only while God was present in that place; once God left, that place ceased to be holy.

When Moses approached the bush, he stepped into holiness. Then, when he departed from that place, he stepped out of holiness. Maybe you feel the same way sometimes. You step into holiness; then you step out of holiness; then you step back into holiness; then you step back out of holiness; then you step into holiness again; then back out again. Sound familiar? Or am I the only conflicted person in the body of Christ?

Far too often, the reality of our Christian experience tends to be a Jekyll-and-Hyde kind of dichotomy in which we spend time in holiness, but then step away and spend whole chunks of time outside holiness. In holiness; out of holiness; in holiness; out of holiness. It's a cycle that frustrates and leaves us with the nagging premonition that we weren't made to live part-time between two different worlds. Jesus didn't die so that we would just visit Him on weekends. He has made provision for us to enter into holiness, to burn with His holy fire of intimate affections, and to stay there. But living 24/7 in holiness sometimes seems more theoretical than practical.

How can we break this cyclical pattern of repeatedly losing our standing in holiness? The answer is found in the blood.

Perfecting Holiness

The blood of Christ has provided for our weakness, even in this struggle to live in the holy place. The blood of Christ covers us while we are on a learning curve to become more and more holy. Paul pointed to this learning curve when he wrote, "...perfecting holiness in the fear of God" (2 Corinthians 7:1). Holiness is something we learn to perfect.

I have not yet perfected holiness. But I'm pursuing this perfection, and here's what I'm finding: I'm spending less and less time away from holiness, and more and more time in the place of holiness. That's what perfecting holiness is all about. It's learning to get sprinkled with blood, enter into the Holiest, and stay, stay, stay there. Spend more time there. Longer chunks of time there. And what about those times we step away from holiness? We perfect holiness by learning how to make those times shorter and shorter. That's done by repenting faster, getting sprinkled with blood, and returning to holiness. We're learning to spend more time *in* the holy place and less time *outside* the holy place—and the whole growing process is covered by the blood.

WHEN I SAW THAT HOLINESS IS A PLACE, THE IDEA OF PERFECTING HOLINESS SUDDENLY BECAME *ATTAINABLE.*

When I saw that holiness is a place, the idea of perfecting holiness suddenly became *attainable.*

If being holy meant adhering perfectly to a list of things that I must not do, I wasn't sure that I would *ever* be holy. *But if holiness is a place, maybe I can get myself in that place. And maybe I can spend more and more time in that place, and less and less time away from it.*

If holiness is a place, it's within reach. I can get there. You can get there. The blood of Christ has guaranteed its attainability. This much I *can* do: I can get in the presence of God!

Highway Of Holiness

I think this is why Isaiah spoke of the walk of holiness as a highway.

A highway shall be there, and a road, and it shall be called the Highway of Holiness. The unclean shall not pass over it, but it shall be for others. Whoever walks the road, although a fool, shall not go astray (Isaiah 35:8).

Holiness is a place—and it's also a journey. In other words, holiness is not a final destination to which we will finally aspire when we die; rather, it's something we can attain even while we're in the process of the journey. It's a path we walk—a very narrow highway—that leads to the holy city, to Zion. The key to holiness is simply this: Stay on the highway. As long as you stay walking on the highway, you're in holiness.

The problem comes when we trip up, lose our focus, and end up in the ditch. It's when we're in the ditch that we must learn what it means to perfect holiness in the fear of the Lord. In a nutshell, it means, "Repent—and get back on the highway."

We learn to perfect holiness by becoming faster repenters. We must learn to decrease the duration of our ditch times. If you land in the ditch (that is, you've stepped out of holiness because of sin), learn the grace of repenting quickly and scrambling back up onto the highway.

By "repenting quickly," I do not mean "repenting superficially." I'm talking about full-blown, heart-wrenching repentance. Just don't stall. Repent hard, repent deeply, repent tearfully—and repent fast.

If you spend less and less time in the ditch, and more and more time on the highway, it means you're perfecting holiness in the fear of the Lord.

> WE LEARN TO PERFECT HOLINESS BY BECOMING FASTER REPENTERS.

Yes, even *you* can be holy! Why? *Because holiness is not a standard of ethical values you must measure up to; rather, it's a place you must enter. It's a highway to stay on, and which will advance you forward into every spiritual blessing.*

Proximity To The Throne

Here's a definition of holiness that I submit for your thoughtful consideration. Holiness is: *Proximity to the throne.*

At the throne of God are myriads of creatures. Some have wings, other's don't. Some have two eyes while others have eyes all over their bodies and even under their wings. Some look like men; others look like animals, such as a lion or a calf; still others look like birds, such as an eagle. Some have been with God longer than others. Those with the greatest honor seem to be those who live closest to God, living inside and around the throne itself. These beings are given various names in Scripture such as angels, cherubim, seraphim, and living creatures. When referring to all of them at once, the Bible uses an interesting phrase. It calls them the "holy ones" (see Daniel 4:17; Job 5:1).

HOLINESS IS PROXIMITY TO THE THRONE.

I want to suggest they're not holy because of *who* they are; they're holy because of *where* they are. They reside in the Holy Place, the place where God dwells, and they are made holy because of their proximity to God.

They're not holy because of who *they* are; they're holy because of who *God* is. They're not holy because of something inherent to *them*, but because of something inherent to *God*. God alone has holiness as an *inherent* attribute. He alone is "The Holy One." All others who surround His throne are holy as a *derived* quality. They derive their holiness from their proximity to The Holy One. Everything close to God is holy. Why? Because God radiates holiness, and everything close to Him becomes holy by virtue of its nearness to Him. In other words, He brings them into that quality or state which enables them to live in His immediate presence without being destroyed.

If you get close enough to God, you too will become holy. Not because of *who* you are, but because of *where* you are. You have received the sprinkling with blood, you have entered with boldness into the throneroom, you have drawn near to God; and now the holiness that defines God's personhood permeates every atom of your being and makes you holy, too. You're holy because you're in the presence of The Holy One.

When you understand this principle, you have no hesitation in saying, "I am a holy man of God," or "I am a holy woman of God." Being "a holy man of God" loses its mystique, its sense of elitist superiority, or the connotation of "exceptional spiritual maturity." I don't call myself holy because I'm impressed with myself. Quite the opposite—I'm profoundly aware of my current struggles. But I'm learning to spend more and more time in the throneroom, and less and less time away from the throneroom. So I'm willing to say in an unabashed, matter-of-fact way, "I'm a holy man of God." Why? Simply because the blood of Christ has brought me into the throneroom of heaven.

IF YOU GET CLOSE ENOUGH TO GOD, YOU TOO WILL BECOME HOLY. NOT BECAUSE OF *WHO* YOU ARE, BUT BECAUSE OF *WHERE* YOU ARE.

Holiness Is A Fire

Some people define as holy the person who has achieved complete victory over the world, the flesh, and the devil. Such a definition makes holiness a formidable mountain that appears almost impossible to climb. If I define holiness as complete spiritual victory, I'll probably see myself as never able to attain it in this life. Holiness, in that distorted model, becomes mostly a list of things that one must not do. "I don't do this, this, this, this, this, this, or this; so therefore, I must be holy." Sorry, Charlie, but your list of all the things you *don't do* isn't able to make you holy.

I'm suggesting that holiness is not so much what I *don't do*, as it is what I *do do*. I get sprinkled with blood, step into the throneroom, and stay there. That's what I do do, and that's what makes me holy.

Holiness is more than simply an absence of defilement. You can focus on cleaning up your act, removing all that defiles, and still not find holiness. Why? *Because holiness is not merely the absence of sin; it's the presence of fire.*

To illustrate, suppose I want to build a bonfire. I gather branches and sticks from the woods and place them in a heap. But the sticks I've collected are muddy and wet. So I take time to clean off the mud and allow the wood to dry out. Eventually I have a pile of wood that is clean and dry. But just because I've gotten rid of everything that could quench the fire does not mean I have a bonfire. Getting rid of the fire-retardants does not give me a bonfire. I don't have a bonfire until there's—fire!

Holiness is a bonfire. (Because our God is a consuming fire.) You can get rid of everything that might extinguish your spiritual flame, but just getting rid of the negative does not mean you're ablaze with holiness. You're not a living bonfire of holiness until you step into the Holiest, get kindled with the living flame upon the altar of God, and burn with a holy fire in the presence of His glorious holiness.

Come with me now as we look at the power of standing in holiness.

Chapter 8

STANDING *in* HOLINESS

"Who may ascend into the hill of the LORD? Or who may stand in His holy place?" (Psalm 24:3). Holiness, for the most part, just stands. Why? Because when you finally attain to the holy place and gaze upon the glorious throne that has fascinated God's holy ones for untold millennia, you are so overwhelmed at the glorious majesty before you that all you care to do is stand and stare.

That's all that the living creatures do: stand and stare. And cry, "Holy, holy, holy!" These amazing creatures whose entire bodies are covered with eyes—eyes represent strength of intelligence, or capacity to comprehend and absorb—can't take their eyes off the throne. The smartest creatures in the universe are utterly consumed with gaping at the boundless wonder of God's matchless works and peerless personhood.

The most pleasurable exhilaration is experienced by the holy ones who stand in the holy place and gaze upon God. Once you attain to this holiness, this will become your chief occupation as well. You will simply want to be found standing and "burning before the throne" (Revelation 4:5). Once you see what they see, you'll stare like they stare.

Jesus revealed that the angels mostly just stand before God. "'Take heed that you do not despise one of these little ones, for I say to you that in heaven their angels always see the face of My Father who is in heaven'" (Matthew 18:10). The angels "always" stand and behold the face of the Father; if the slightest hint of displeasure crosses His face, His angels will be dispatched with vengeance against those who despise His little ones.

Gabriel the archangel, when he appeared to Zacharias, described his occupation in this manner: "'I am Gabriel, who stands in the presence of God'" (Luke 1:19).

"So what do you do, Gabriel?"

"I stand in the presence of God."

"Yes, I understand that, but I'm wondering what you do."

"I stand in the presence of God."

"Yes, I get that, but I mean, you're an angel; so what exactly does an angel *do*?"

"I'm not sure you're hearing me," I can imagine an exasperated Gabriel retorting. "That's what I *do*. I stand in the presence of God, gape with wonder at His glory, and burn with fiery desire before the throne. If He sends me somewhere, I go; if He doesn't send me, I just stand there."

Gabriel appeared three times in Scripture. He first appeared to Daniel; then roughly 600 years later he appeared to Zacharias; and then six months later he came to Mary. That was the busy season. What was Gabriel doing during all those "silent" centuries? Standing in holiness.

The goal of my life is to be found standing in holiness. The hosts of heaven stand before "the Lord of hosts." I consider myself just one member of heaven's hosts (armies). It's my privilege, as part of heaven's hosts, to stand before God in holiness, and then one day to be found in His triumphal train as He rides forth with heaven's armies to reclaim this planet as His own (Revelation 19:14).

To Be Found Standing

On one occasion, the great Persian king Ahasuerus had a sudden urge to expedite a certain matter in his kingdom. It was an unpremeditated, spontaneous decision. When the urge hit him, he immediately realized he needed a servant to expedite the matter on his behalf. So he quickly asked his servants who attended him, "'Who is in the court?'" (see Esther 6:1-4).

The king had an outer court in which people would stand and wait when they wanted an audience with him. If the king was willing to see them, he would call for them. Until called for, these supplicants would just wait in the court, hoping for a hearing. So the king was asking, "Is there anyone standing in the court, waiting for me to call on them?"

THE ONE WHO IS FOUND STANDING IN HOLINESS WHEN THE KING WANTS SOMETHING DONE WILL GET THE ASSIGNMENT.

The servants replied, "Yes, there's one man standing in the court, waiting on you." His name was Haman, and he was an evil man. Since he was the one standing in the court when the king had a sudden brainchild, he was the one who was commissioned with the king's task. I'm not defending Haman here, he was an evil man. The point I'm making is, he got the job because he was found standing in the court when the king wanted something done.

When the King of the universe wants to do something, He asks the question, "Who is in the court?" What He is asking is, "Who is in My court, standing in holiness, waiting on Me, available to Me for any Kingdom purpose?" The one who is found standing in holiness when the King wants something done will get the assignment.

I see this truth illustrated in the life of Saul of Tarsus. God had tackled Saul while he was on a road trip to Damascus, arrested him, and now needed a servant to go to Saul and prophesy to him his calling as an apostle of the Lamb. Which servant could He send to Saul? Bear with my imagination as I paint a scenario of how it could have possibly come down.

God turns to an angel and asks, "Who is in the court? Send someone to check out Damascus. Is there anyone in Damascus who is standing in the court? Find someone who is standing in holiness, ministering to Me, and available for service."

A posse of angels is immediately dispatched to scope out Damascus. Soon, the angel at God's side is reporting their findings. "Your Majesty, we have scouted out Damascus, and I hate to say this, but there is no one standing in the court in Damascus. In fact, everything in Damascus is disrupted right now. You see, when the believers heard that Saul of Tarsus was coming to town with legal authority to imprison anyone confessing the Lord Jesus, things got real chaotic. About half the believers left town. Some of them renounced their faith. Some went into hiding. Others are trembling in the corners of their houses. But as far as finding anyone who has not been moved, anyone who is simply standing in Your courts and ministering to—um, excuse me, Your Honor. Wait a moment, I have an incoming call."

The angel cocks his head to listen more closely to his earpiece. He's getting an update from the ground troops in Damascus. "What's that? You say you've found someone in the court? There's a man standing in the court? Well, what's his name?"

Turning to the throne, the angel reports, "Your Honor, as it turns out, there's still one man standing in the court. They tell me his name is Ananias. Have You ever heard of him?"

"Yes, I've heard of him."

"Well, Ananias is the only one in all of Damascus who is still standing in the holy place. Would You like to send him to Saul?"

"Yes, send Ananias. He'll do."

Obviously the above conversation is fictitious, but my point is this: Ananias got the privilege of commissioning Paul to his apostolic ministry because he was found standing in the court when the King needed a servant. During his lifetime of service, Ananias was going to have one shot at greatness. *If he would be found standing in holiness at the right moment, he would be commissioned with the defining task of his life.*

This is why sprinkling with blood is so important to me. I get sprinkled with blood every day so that I might stand in holiness in the courts of the King and be available to Him for anything He might need that day. *Perhaps my entire life existence, like that of Ananias's, will be defined by one moment in time when I was found standing in holiness.*

The Authority Of Holiness

Holiness makes us available in service to God. Those who stand before God in this manner carry with them an unmistakable bearing of spiritual authority.

Holy men and women of God, while appearing quite ordinary on the outside, have an inner reality in God that gives them authority with men, with hell, and also with heaven. There are many church leaders who desire to have authority when they stand before people; but who will seek to have authority when they stand in the presence of God?

The only way to gain authority with God is to get sprinkled with blood and then stand before Him in holiness. This is what gives angels their authority. They stand and behold the face of the Father (Matthew 18:10), which places them in a position to be sent on any mission at a moment's notice. Thus, standing in holiness gives them great authority in heaven.

Holy people also have authority with men. Speaking of John the Baptist, Mark 6:20 says, "Herod feared John, knowing that he *was* a just and holy man." King Herod didn't fear John merely because he was just (righteous). There are blameless people out there, but they don't necessarily carry any unusual authority about them. John had an authority that caused the king to fear, not so much because he was a *just* man, but because he was a *holy* man. John was a man who stood in the courts of the King and burned with a holy fire. Herod probably didn't have accurate language for it, but he perceived there was something different about John, and it made him tremble. John had authority with the king because he stood in holiness.

Holy men and women have authority with heaven and authority with men; and they also have authority with hell. For example, when the demons recognized Christ's authority over them, they cried out, "'Let us alone! What have we to do with You, Jesus of Nazareth? Did You come to destroy us? I know who You are—*the Holy One of God!*'" (Mark 1:24). The demons perceived Jesus' holiness and knew He had authority over them.

Standing in holiness has the potential to grant you authority in heaven, on the earth, and under the earth. This is why your enemy targets your holiness so relentlessly. The scheme of darkness against every single saint, when all the trappings are removed, is focused strategically on one specific pinpoint: "Get him out of holiness!" "Get her out of holiness!"

Your enemy knows that if he can get you to compromise your holiness, you will sacrifice your authority with men, with heaven, and with hell. *The battle of the ages, therefore, is for the high ground of holiness.*

There is no one more dangerous to the designs of darkness than the man or woman who has learned to get sprinkled with blood and stand in the holy place before the Lord of the universe. These are the saints who rewrite human history.

Noah became a historymaker by standing in holiness while staring down the taunting sneers of a reviling, unbelieving generation.

Job became a historymaker by standing in holiness while enduring the most horrific nightmare Satan could concoct in his hellish laboratory.

Abraham became a historymaker by standing in holiness even when every natural indicator told him it was impossible for God's promise to be fulfilled in his life.

Joseph became a historymaker by standing in holiness in the face of Potiphar's wife's seductions, and in the suffocating clutch of an old-world, lice-infested, Egyptian prison.

Naomi became a historymaker by standing in holiness through the grinding grief of losing her husband and then both her sons.

Hannah became a historymaker by standing in holiness even though her rival incessantly provoked her with malicious reminders of her barrenness.

David became a historymaker by standing in holiness even while he fled from Saul for his life, living every day with "'but a step between [him] and death'" (1 Samuel 20:3).

Jeremiah became a historymaker by standing in holiness despite tortures from venomous leaders who viewed him as an unpatriotic Babylon-lover.

Zacharias became a historymaker by standing in

holiness regardless of the fact that God had seemingly denied his life-dominating prayer for a son. Decades of heartsickness over unanswered prayer had so encrusted his spirit that even when he received a personal visitation by the radiating archangel Gabriel, he was unable to transition over into faith. The ten months of muteness was God's way to put Zacharias on the fast track into faith. After the crucible of affliction, Zacharias emerged with a stunning prophetic anointing that empowered him to raise his epoch-shifting son, John the Baptist.

The thing that qualified Zacharias for historymaking was not his faith—he failed on that score. It was his (and Elizabeth's) holiness (Luke 1:6). We're looking at a dynamic here that warrants us revisiting a verse mentioned in the previous chapter.

> A highway shall be there, and a road, and it shall be called the Highway of Holiness. The unclean shall not pass over it, but it shall be for others. Whoever walks the road, although a fool, shall not go astray (Isaiah 35:8).

Isaiah mentions "a fool" in this verse. I want to draw a connection between "a fool" and "an unbeliever." The primary essence of foolishness is *unbelief*. (See Psalm 14:1 and Luke 24:25.) There is nothing more foolish than to disbelieve any word that proceeds from the mouth of the living God. Isaiah is saying it's possible to be a fool (someone who is in unbelief) and still be walking "the Highway of Holiness."

I hear Isaiah saying, "Even if you're struggling with the foolishness of unbelief, stay on the Highway of Holiness. If you will just stay in holiness, you will not go astray and miss your destiny. Whatever you do, hold to your holiness! Because if you do, even if you are assailed by the winds of doubt and perplexity, the Highway of

Holiness will lead you forward into the sunshine of God's intended destiny for your life."

Although a fool (because he succumbed to unbelief), Zacharias stayed on the Highway of Holiness and eventually emerged into his ultimate destiny.

Jesus Christ became a Historymaker by standing in holiness through the darkest ordeal any man has ever endured. The greatest war ever won was fought by a Man who just stood on the nail and burned with holy love.

Today's historymakers are forged the same way. The greatness of your trial becomes an invitation to change history. Draw your line in the sand. If you will resolve to stand in holiness before your God with the lovesick gaze of mesmerized affection, nothing can deter you from attaining your destination on this Highway of Holiness. The proclamation uttered over Daniel is yours to claim as well, "'Your God, whom you serve continually, He will deliver you'" (Daniel 6:16).

> NOTHING CAN DETER YOU FROM ATTAINING YOUR DESTINATION ON THIS HIGHWAY OF HOLINESS.

I Shall Not Be Moved

Let's go back and consider the stunning testimony of Psalm 15.

> LORD, who may abide in Your tabernacle? Who may dwell in Your holy hill? He who walks uprightly, and works righteousness, and speaks the truth in his heart...He who does these things shall never be moved (Psalm 15:1-2,5),

This Psalm declares that the one who lives in the presence of God and dwells in the holy place "shall never be moved." Stand in holiness and nothing can move you. Ever.

In Psalm 86:1-2, David used three adjectives to describe his condition: "poor," "needy," and "holy." Being poor and needy did not disqualify him from being holy. Quite the contrary. It was because he was poor and needy that he clung to his holiness. Poverty and neediness didn't dislodge him from holiness; they strengthened his resolve to stay in holiness. Nothing was permitted to move him!

Not everyone reading these words is aware of my personal trial. In 1992, my world suddenly collapsed when I was struck by a vocal injury. It came upon me like a snare upon an unsuspecting bird. I underwent surgery for a problem in the area of my larynx, but the surgery went bad. My vocal strength declined with usage until I was left with perhaps 5% of my vocal ability. I have significant pain levels whenever I attempt to use the little voice that I have. Above all, I am clinging fervently to God's many promises related to my healing.

During the wait, my life has become a string of resignations. I am a lot of "former" things: a former pastor; a former worship leader; a former president, etc. I struggled for years to remain faithful to my ministry callings, but as my voice grew steadily weaker, I was slowly squeezed out of the ministries I loved. Eventually, I was forced to resign our pastorate in upstate New York. In the spring of 1999, we moved 1,100 miles across the plains of America to Kansas City, Missouri, where we now enjoy our partnership with the International House Of Prayer (ihop.org). As I write this, 16 years after the initial injury, I am able to maintain a light speaking load, traveling most weekends to minister to the body of Christ. But my primary focus is on living a life of prayer and praise, burning in holiness before the throne of God, and waiting on Him in faith to send from heaven and save me (Psalm 57:3).

That quick snapshot on my infirmity will help you understand my next point. When I was in Psalm 15, and saw that the one who dwells in God's holy hill shall never be moved, I began to have a quiet argument with the Lord. I said in my heart, "Lord, I don't get this verse. It says that your holy one shall never be moved. I've held tenaciously to holiness, but I've been moved during these past 16 years from just about everything I ever knew. I've been moved from the titles I held, from the offices I filled, from the ministries in which I served, and from most of the relationships I once enjoyed. And besides all that, I've been moved 1,100 miles from beautiful upstate New York to *Missouri* of all places! How can You say, 'He shall not be moved'? I've been moved from just about *everything!*"

Softly, the question came back, "Have you been moved from before My throne?"

Instantly, that question answered everything for me.

"O Abba," I replied, "As long as You help me, I shall *never* be moved from before Your throne! I am resolved now, more than ever, to stand before You in holiness. Having done all to stand, I will continue to stand before You. This is the most important thing in my life. By Your grace, nothing shall move me."

Now that I'm standing here, in the holy place, you can't trip me, or stop me, or frighten, entice, tempt, interrupt, hinder, distract, detour, derail, deter, disorient, or dissuade me. I am immovable in holiness.

You can take away my titles, you can take away my ministry, you can remove me from the platform, you can take away my song, you can take away my friends, and you can take away my voice. But there's one thing you can't take from me. You can't take away my holiness. As long as I live, I am resolved to stand before my Beloved, give Him the deepest affections of my heart, and burn before Him with the holy fires of lovesickness and heart-sickness. I shall not be moved!

Holiness Will Rise Again

You can bury a holy man or woman of God under a mountain of grief and heartache, but when that man or woman clings to holiness, he or she cannot be held captive by "so great a death" (2 Corinthians 1:10), but will surely rise up in the salvation of the Lord.

Go ahead, Satan, and bury Job under a mountain of grief. The only problem is, you've buried a holy man of God who refuses to be moved from before the throne. You cannot keep this holy man buried forever; eventually, he will rise and do great damage to your kingdom because of the testimony of an overcoming life.

Go ahead, Satan, and bury Joseph in a stale, stinky, Egyptian prison. But you've made a strategic error be-cause you've buried one of God's holy ones. This coffin cannot hold a holy man of God. You can't keep holiness buried forever. The longer you try to hold him down, the higher he'll rise. Keep Joseph in slavery and imprisonment for ten years, and he will rise to the throne of the land.

Go ahead, Satan, and bury Elizabeth under a moun-tain of sorrow and reproach (because of childlessness). But you've made another strategic error—you've buried a holy woman of God. Elizabeth has kept herself "blame-less" in holiness (Luke 1:6), and holiness cannot remain shackled forever in this prison of barrenness. When God resurrects her, it will not simply be into motherhood, but He will make her the mother of the greatest prophet ever (John the Baptist).

Romans 1:4 says that the Lord Jesus was "declared to be the Son of God with power according to the Spirit of holiness, by the resurrection from the dead." In other words, it was Christ's *holiness* that precipitated His resurrection. This truth was prophesied in David, "For You will not leave my soul in Sheol, nor will You allow Your *Holy One* to see corruption" (Psalm 16:10). That verse applies initially to David, who was buried under a heap of heartache and distress while he ran from Saul for his life. David was resurrected from his ghastly wilderness because of his holiness. But Psalm 16:10 is actually speaking of Christ Jesus, who did not see corruption. Jesus' body experienced rigor mortis, but it never experienced corruption because He rose before decay set in.

Go ahead, Satan, and bury Jesus Christ in a tomb. Now, *that's* a major strategic error! You've just buried Holiness Himself! The grave could not contain Holiness. On the third day, Jesus rose from the grave and was raised by the Father to the highest place.

> Therefore God also has highly exalted Him and given Him the name which is above every name, that at the name of Jesus every knee should bow, of those in heaven, and of those on earth, and of those under the earth, and that every tongue should confess that Jesus Christ is Lord, to the glory of God the Father (Philippians 2:9-11).

It was true of David and of Christ, and it's also true of you! The adversary can't keep holiness buried forever. Even if you feel dead and buried under the weight of God's disciplining hand, devote yourself to His holy presence. Regardless of your shattered dreams and deferred hopes, get sprinkled with the blood every day and live in the bosom of the Father. As you love Him from your grave, you are robbing Satan of his agenda for your

THE ADVERSARY CAN'T KEEP HOLINESS BURIED FOREVER.

life, and releasing God's agenda for your life.

Remain in holiness and Psalm 91 becomes the prophetic declaration of Jesus Christ over your life:

> "Because he has set his love upon Me,
> therefore I will deliver him; I will set him on
> high, because he has known My name. He
> shall call upon Me, and I will answer him; I
> will be with him in trouble; I will deliver him
> and honor him. With long life I will satisfy
> him, and show him My salvation" (Psalm
> 91:14-16).

If you feel you've been consigned to a hell all your own, let me offer some advice based on Romans 1:4: Bring holiness into your hell. It's inevitable—*holiness will rise again!*

Never Rule Out Holiness

You might see a saint who appears to be knocked out of the race, but if that saint is living in holiness, don't rule him out too hastily. Because if he resolves to stay in holiness, his story's not finished. That's what Micah was affirming when he confessed, "Therefore I will look to the Lord; I will wait for the God of my salvation; my God will hear me. Do not rejoice over me, my enemy; when I fall, I will arise; when I sit in darkness, the Lord will be a light to me" (Micah 7:7-8). *As long as you're standing here, sprinkled with the blood of the Lamb, accepted by the Father, and burning in holiness, your story's not over.* It's never too late for holiness to be exonerated.

BRING HOLINESS
INTO YOUR HELL.

If you've fallen into a Joseph-like pit, one reason may be because God is wanting to write a story with your life. God always writes the best stories with His holy ones.

Could it be that it was because of your holiness that Satan targeted you? Could it be that it's because of your holiness that God will reverse and redeem all that the enemy intended for evil, and turn it into good?

God: Storyteller Par Excellence

Let me tell you a bit more about my story. I'm a PK (preacher's kid), raised by godly parents who modeled authenticity and integrity. Family altar was as standard to our morning as breakfast (Sunday being the only exception because we went to Sunday School and church). I was taught to pray from the moment I could repeat the simplest words. During my childhood I responded to so many altar calls that I don't know when I was actually saved. I don't remember a time when I didn't love Jesus.

GOD DOESN'T WRITE SHORT STORIES.

Never, even in my teen years, did I rebel or turn away from my Lord. When asked to give my testimony, I would hesitate and begin to mumble. "Well, I was raised in a Christian home...um...I was baptized in the Holy Spirit at age nine...uh...I've loved the Lord all my life..." In two minutes my story was done.

"My testimony is boring," I told the Lord.

It's as though He shot back, "We can change that." Since 1992, I've been profoundly aware that God is writing a story with my life.

God's a great Author, and He loves to write stories with the lives of His holy ones. Not skinny, thin little booklets; He doesn't write short stories. He likes to write fat books that testify to the greatness of His salvation and the grandeur of His name.

I've discovered something about God: He's got a flair for the dramatic. If it's a choice between black-and-white and color, He goes with the colorful version. God doesn't stay in the center lane; He flirts with precipices. His symphonies start out with violinic serenity, but before they're done He's churning an armada of timpani into a thunderous crescendo.

Look at Peter, for example. Peter was in Herod's prison for a number of days, but when did God decide to liberate Peter from prison? The very morning that Herod was intending to execute him. God could have delivered him days earlier, but He waited till the last moment.

Why is He sometimes a last-minute God? Why does he stall on intervention until the tension becomes gargantuan? Why does He wait to help His people until "the break of dawn"? (Psalm 46:5). I mean, look at how He wrote the symphony of Israel's exodus from Egypt. Talk about sensational! He just kept intensifying the pressure on Pharaoh and all of Egypt and Israel until it seemed everybody would explode. Finally, Pharaoh let God's people go—only to change his mind and chase them into the sea. The whole ordeal is so very dramatic. And what a fantastic climax! Pharaoh and his army end up as bloated corpses on the beach. There's no getting around it, God likes to make big, dramatic splashes that culminate in magnificent demonstrations of His mighty salvation.

Little wonder Solomon wrote, "Blessed be the Lord God, the God of Israel, who only does wondrous things!" (Psalm 72:18). That's all God *ever* does—wondrous things. If it's not wondrous, He didn't do it. And if He did it, it'll leave you marveling in gaping admiration.

Psalm 92:7 tells us that God purposely exalts the wicked so that the calamity of their fall will be all the greater. But He does the exact opposite with His holy ones. *He orchestrates the extremity of their humiliation so that the glory of their exaltation shines all the brighter.*

When I finally realized the Author of faith was setting me up to obtain a good testimony, I began to complain, "Lord, if You're writing a story with my life, then can we get on with it? Hurry up! This is taking forever!"

God's answer was, "I call fast boring." Turns out He likes a good plot. He's not interested in making your life a flash-in-the-pan, BOOM-it's-over kind of explosion that's over as fast as it came. No, He intends to savor every phase of your journey. He says, "I'm going to write some suspense into your story. A little bit of intrigue. A little bit of mystery. A good dose of romance." (Because by the time you're done, you're going to come out of the thing totally enthralled with the beauty of the Lord Jesus.) "I'll take you through the valley of the shadow of death. You'll engage in hand-to-hand combat with the enemy. You'll smell demons' breath. At times you'll feel like you're careening past the cliffs of Hades. But if you'll stay in the secret place of the Most High, I'll bring you through to rich fulfillment."

In the end, you will stand in the "great cloud of witnesses" (Hebrews 12:1), raise your hands to the One you love, and testify through tears of gratitude, "He was faithful to finish what He started in my life. His grace *was* sufficient for me. He who is mighty has done great things for me, and I am glad! Holy is His name!"

When we are gathered around the throne with the saints of all the ages, and we begin to share our stories about the goodness of God, every one of us will want to have a story to tell. We'll rejoice in others' testimonies, but just listening to others won't satisfy us. It won't be good enough that Joseph has a great story to tell. When we get to the other side, we'll want a story of

I DON'T WANT JOSEPH TO BE THE ONLY ONE WITH A GREAT STORY.

our own! We'll want to be able to say, "Sit down and listen for a while, and let me tell you about the time..."

Therefore, we shall not be moved. We will get sprinkled with blood every day, take our stand at the throne of God, burn with holiness in the courts of the King, and wait on Him until He proves Himself the Finisher of our faith.

"'He who is holy, let him be holy still'" (Revelation 22:11).

Amen.

Chapter 9

THE WAR *to* REMAIN *in* HOLINESS

The primary battleground in every believer's life is the fight to remain in holiness. Satan will do everything in his power to move us from holiness, so in this chapter I want to deal with how he goes about it. It's essential that we understand our enemy's schemes because, when we understand the nature of the war, we are empowered to withstand more effectively.

God Brought David Into Holiness

David was a man who stepped into holiness in a way that was very uncommon for his dispensation. He lived during a time when the way into the Holiest was cordoned off by a heavy, curtain-like veil. Only the high priest was to enter behind the veil into the Holiest, and that just once a year. The veil signified this message: "The way into the Holiest of All has not yet been made manifest. When that way is manifest, the veil will be torn, indicating that all can now have access to the Holiest through the blood of the Lamb." (See Hebrews 9:7-8.)

Throughout his upbringing, David's only paradigm for approaching God was Moses' tabernacle. Ordinary people couldn't gaze upon Holiness (the ark) because it was intentionally hidden by God behind a veil. Since Moses' law mandated that the ark remain behind the veil, David must have been startled when the Holy Spirit revealed to him, perhaps through Samuel or Nathan, that God was inviting him to approach Him under an entirely new paradigm.

However He communicated it to David, God basically said, "David, I'm inviting you into a unique dimension of intimacy with Me, and here's how I want you to come into it. I want you to find the ark of the covenant and bring it to Zion. But instead of placing it behind a veil or curtain, I want you to build a tabernacle for it, and then position the ark in open view. Then, I want you to come and sit before the ark, draw near to Me, gaze on My glory, cultivate a fiery spirit of love, and burn before Me in holiness."

THE PRIMARY BATTLE-GROUND IN EVERY BELIEVER'S LIFE IS THE FIGHT TO REMAIN IN HOLINESS.

What an invitation! God was giving David an entirely new paradigm of what it meant to approach Him and worship Him in the beauties of holiness. He didn't realize it but, by placing himself before the ark in this manner, he became a prophetic symbol of the kind of approach God was preparing for His people. The time would come when men would be able to approach God, not through a veil of cloth, but through the veil of Christ's flesh (Hebrews 10:20), made acceptable to God by the sprinkling of Christ's blood.

How Did David Do It?

David would start by grabbing his guitar (well, okay, it was a harp—but his harp was the equivalent of today's guitar). He would bring the guitar into the tabernacle, seat himself in front of the ark, and gaze into the glory of God that dwelt upon the ark. Then, as he strummed the guitar, he would start stepping out into prophetic song, singing praises spontaneously to the One he loved. As he sang, the river of love would begin to flow in his spirit, and he would begin to soar in the psalmist anointing. It was here that some of his best psalms were composed.

I can't prove this, but I'm convinced David would also bring portions of the Law (the Torah, the books of Moses), open them up before him, and sing from the Scriptures as he meditated in the Law of God. I have yet another personal theory about David: I think his favorite book was Deuteronomy. "Why Deuteronomy?" you might ask. Because when you see some of the words that are used in Deuteronomy, and then come over to the Psalms, you find the vocabulary of Deuteronomy all through the Psalms.

In Deuteronomy, for example, you find one place where God is called King; then, when you flip over to Psalms, you see it everywhere: King, King, King, King.

In Deuteronomy, God is called the Rock; in Psalms, David calls Him "my rock" over and over.

In Deuteronomy, there's one verse that refers to God as our shield. David peered into that truth about God as he played before the ark, and as a result he wrote many songs that talked about God as our shield.

In Deuteronomy, you find just one verse that calls God our refuge. Check out the Psalms and it's everywhere— refuge, refuge, refuge. Why? Because David would meditate in the truths of the Law, allow them to expand in his understanding as he worshiped before the ark, and then he would write down the inspired songs the Holy Spirit gave him.

This was David's way of digging deep into the rich deposits of God's word. He would follow a lode of revelation, mining from a verse everything he could uncover, and then he would expound in song his insight into that

Scripture. As he used the word to empower his worship and intercession, his heart would overflow with fiery love, and he would stand before God and burn in the place of holiness. Guitar...Torah...ark...gazing...intimacy...fire... holiness...lovesickness...psalm-writing...weeping... This was the one thing David came to live for (Psalm 27:4).

The Assault Upon David

When David found this holy place, he became dangerous to the kingdom of darkness. So Satan pulled out his best strategies to try to move David from holiness.

Satan has three primary strategies to move the saint of God from the place of holiness: distraction, discouragement, and temptation. These three battlefronts are as common to man today as they were thousands of years ago. They summarize the primary battle in the life of every person reading these words.

Distraction, discouragement, and temptation—those are the three biggies. After studying the vulnerabilities of the human frame for centuries, Satan has fine-tuned how he assaults God's people and narrowed it down to three basic strategies. One of those three is probably your major battleground right now. Mind you, if you stay with us long enough, you'll experience all three.

SATAN HAS THREE PRIMARY STRATEGIES TO MOVE THE SAINT OF GOD FROM THE PLACE OF HOLINESS: DISTRACTION, DISCOURAGEMENT, AND TEMPTATION.

(a) Distraction.

Satan sought to move David from holiness by distracting him with overwhelming demands. Satan doesn't mind if David receives a promotion to the throne because, even though it means he will have a larger sphere of influence among people, it also means that he will likely be bombarded with all kinds of new demands upon his time and attention. The new and pressing responsibilities have the result, in most cases, of distracting God's servant from his primary commitment to abiding in the place of holiness. Thus distracted, the effectiveness of God's servant is significantly compromised. This strategy is effective in the majority of cases, so Satan is willing to gamble that David will be just like the other guys. His plan is that David will be swept up in the time demands of busywork and sacrifice his commitment to spend time burning in holiness. Your enemy knows that holiness, above all, requires time. You can't live in holiness on the run.

What was David's response? I can imagine David saying to the nation's leaders, "You're telling me you want me to be your king. But are you sure? I need to tell you who I am, so that if you get me as king you understand what you're getting. I'm a guy who lives for only one thing. There's one thing I've asked of the Lord, and this is what I seek, that I may dwell in the house of the Lord all the days of my life. My primary life vision is to gaze upon the beauty of the Lord and to ask Him questions while I'm in His presence, waiting on Him to hear His voice. So if you're willing for *that* kind of package to be your king, then I'm willing to serve. But if you want someone who will become servant to all the demands that vie for the attention of a nation's leader, then I'm not your guy."

The people chose to install David as king, and Satan did his utmost to distract David and weaken his spirit. David, however, refused to allow distraction to move him from holiness.

(b) Discouragement.

Wow, discouragement can be almost overwhelming at times. Demonic powers seem to have studied the art of assaulting God's servants with discouragement, oppression, and depression. If there's anything Satan is experienced at, it's introducing lies and doubt and unbelief into the thought life of believers. He seeks to convince us that God is not going to work on our behalf this time around, and that this thing is going from bad to worse. Satan tries to make us feel trapped, helpless, hopeless, alone, discarded by God, and without recourse. His croaky voice whispers, "Nothing is going to change. Except for the worse."

The enemy used discouragement against David more than once. When David was hiding out in forests and wildernesses and caves, running for his life from Saul, he battled discouragement on virtually a daily basis. He was constantly fighting to encourage himself in the Lord.

David chose the right response to discouragement: he devoted himself to prayer and holiness. David chose the response that Jesus Himself modeled for us because when Jesus was hit with discouragement He went to the place of prayer. The more He hurt, the more He prayed. And when He *really* hurt, He prayed even harder (Luke 22:44).

This is the path the ancients walked. When they were assaulted with discouragement, they prayed. I'm talking about prayer that is aided and lubricated by fasting and meditation in the word. David got on that ancient path and prayed his way through to victory. And he did it over and over. That's why his psalms carry such power for us still today. Many of them were birthed through his struggles with discouragement and depression. *Now, as we pray and sing our way through David's psalms, we gain strength and grace to resist the stench of the dragon's breath.* Not only do we overcome in the battle, we're made stronger for it. The things we learned in our struggle are now being used to empower other believers in their battles with discouragement. We're not only conquerors over the enemy's onslaught, we're "more than conquerors"

(Romans 8:37)—we've emerged from the battle even more dangerous to the kingdom of darkness than when we went in.

Satan did his utmost to discourage David, but David refused to allow his struggles with discouragement to move him from the place of holiness. He persevered in holiness in the face of both distraction and discouragement.

Now we come to Satan's third tactic: Temptation.

(c) Temptation.

Here's where David's story took a most unfortunate turn. Distraction and discouragement didn't sideline David, but temptation proved to be his nemesis.

David's Battle With Temptation

Without question, David was in Satan's cross hairs. As long as David lived in the place of holiness, he was a threat to the ambitions of darkness. Satan was doubtless waiting, therefore, for the perfect opportunity to exploit the sinfulness of David's flesh. Finally, the right moment presented itself.

David just happened to look out from his palace one day and saw Bathsheba bathing. Lust conceived in his heart and gave birth to sin (James 1:15). David ended up committing adultery with her. Then, when he learned that she had become pregnant from their tryst, he devised a plan to cover up their adultery. His plan seemed to work. He murdered Bathsheba's husband, Uriah, married her, and thus became the "legitimate" father of the child she was carrying. Nobody knew otherwise.

Nobody, that is, except God. And Satan. And David.

Satan's scheme had been successful. David had been sidelined, knocked out of the place of holiness. David knew it. And so did God.

That's why God, in His mercy, sent Nathan to David

to confront him with his sin. God wanted to restore David to holiness. When Nathan confronted David, David confessed his sin openly and repented passionately before God.

I have a personal theory about this story. I think David was *over-ripe* to repent. When Nathan finally confronted him, I think David was *intensely* relieved to stop the charade, repent, and be restored to his Father's arms. Why do I think that? Because when you've ONCE YOU'VE KNOWN known the exhilaration of burning THE THRILL OF HOLINESS, YOU MAKE A in holiness, and then lose it, you are WRETCHED SINNER. absolutely *miserable*. Once you've known the thrill of holiness, you're ruined for ever. What I mean is, you're never again able to enjoy sin. You make a wretched sinner. You've known the wonder of gazing upon His holiness, and now the bankrupt counterfeits of sin are never again able to satisfy.

The Terror Of A Quenched Spirit

Before he repented, I can imagine David trying to return to holiness by his own efforts. He picks up his guitar, enters the tabernacle, sits before the ark, and shakes himself. "Wow, that was a bad month! Whew! I need to shake that off. That was nothing short of a nightmare. I'm going to put that behind me and press forward. It's time to hit the delete button. Aarghh. Okay. Just forget about the whole thing. I'm picking up and moving on. I just need to sing and worship and get back to where I was."

So he hits a chord on his guitar, peers forward at the ark of the covenant, and tries to sing. *Paste*. It feels like paste in his mouth. His tongue won't work right. "Man, this is tough!" He strums a few more chords. Nothing is moving.

"Tomorrow. I need to come back tomorrow," David

thinks to himself. "I need a little more time."

He comes back the next day. He sits down, gazes at the ark, hits a chord on his guitar, and tries to worship. "I love You, Lord! I love You with all my heart. Lord, You *know* I love You!" This time he stays with it longer. He's trying to fan the flame. He's desperate to have the old fire back in his spirit. He sings through one of his favorite psalms, the one that always set his heart on fire in the past.

Nothing.

"Tomorrow! I think if I just relax a bit and come back tomorrow, it will be a new day."

He returns the next day to once again sit before the ark. *Strum, strum, strum.* Nothing. This time his heart starts to pound in his chest and he begins to panic. "Oh no! I've lost it! I've lost the fire! What am I going to do?"

You see, David had known the exhilaration of worshiping in holiness. He had known the joy of having a river of holy love course through his being, igniting new songs within his spirit, and expanding his knowledge of his beloved Lord. Now, the fire was gone! He was successful in hiding his sin from the public, but he couldn't pretend with God. He had lost the most precious thing in his life, and I'm persuaded he was desperate to get it back.

That's why I believe that when Nathan confronted him, David's response was probably something like, "Thank you, thank you, thank you! O how I've needed to repent! I needed your help, Nathan. Thank you for being faithful and delivering the word of the Lord. I've missed the glory of God's holy fire in my spirit, and I am so ready to confess my sin and return to Him."

Restoration To Holiness

When David repented of his sin, he wrote one of the most moving psalms in your Bible. I'm referring to Psalm 51, the psalm he wrote at the time he repented of his adultery and murder. Here's a brief excerpt.

> Create in me a clean heart, O God, and renew a steadfast spirit within me. Do not cast me away from Your presence, and do not take Your Holy Spirit from me. Restore to me the joy of Your salvation, and uphold me by Your generous Spirit (Psalm 51:10-12).

In Psalm 51, David coined a term that appears for the very first time in Scripture. When a word or phrase appears for the first time in the Bible, it is deserving of special attention because it constitutes the cornerstone occurrence of that truth. Every other occurrence of that truth in Scripture builds upon the precedent established by that initial mention.

Up until Psalm 51, every designation of the Third Person of the Godhead was expressed as "the Spirit," or "the Spirit of God," or "the Spirit of the Lord." But now, for the first time ever, David cries out, "Do not take Your *Holy* Spirit from me." David was the first one to call the Spirit of God the *Holy Spirit*. Here's how I imagine David explaining his revelation into this appellation for God's Spirit.

"When I stepped away from holiness by falling to temptation, I lost the fire in my heart and the Spirit departed from me. When the Spirit left, I knew it was because I had compromised my holiness. That's when I realized that He is, above and beyond all else, a *Holy* Spirit."

Little wonder David went on to pray, "Oh God, please do not ever again remove Your Holy Spirit from my life! The reason I live is to worship in Your presence with Your holy fire. Without Your Holy Spirit ablaze in my spirit, life is not worth living. So whatever You do—however You decide to discipline me for my sin—please don't take Your Holy Spirit away from me!"

God Wants To Restore You!

If David could counsel us from heaven today, I think he would say something like, *"There's nothing worth losing your fire!* Take it from me, a guy who had it and then lost it. I paid an agonizing price for the wisdom that I am now sharing with you. The passing pleasures of sin were not worth what I lost. We're made to burn before God with a holy fire, and there's nothing worth losing that."

> WE'RE MADE TO BURN BEFORE GOD WITH A HOLY FIRE, AND THERE'S NOTHING WORTH LOSING THAT.

The first observation to be made regarding David's failure is this: There were consequences for his sin. He paid dearly for it, especially in his family. Nathan told David of the unfortunate consequences that would follow, even though his sin was forgiven.

> "'Now therefore, the sword shall never depart from your house, because you have despised Me, and have taken the wife of Uriah the Hittite to be your wife.' Thus says the LORD: 'Behold, I will raise up adversity against you from your own house; and I will take your wives before your eyes and give them to your neighbor, and he shall lie with your wives in the sight of this sun. For you did it secretly, but I will do this thing before all Israel, before the sun.'" So David said to Nathan, "I have sinned against the LORD." And Nathan said to David, "The LORD also has put away your sin; you shall not die. However, because by this deed you have given great occasion to the enemies of the LORD to blaspheme, the child also who is born to you shall surely die" (2 Samuel 12:10-14).

We see, then, that sinful failure is no small thing, and we should tremble in godly fear of even coming *close* to crossing the line.

The second observation to be made about David's failure is this: David's sin and subsequent restoration are a compelling testimony to the grace and mercy of God. David's life tells us that even when we fail, we never fall so low that God cannot pick us up and restore us. David had become a *murderer* and *adulterer*, and yet God restored him to holiness. David's story encourages our hearts as we grapple with our own deficiencies and tendencies to wander. His testimony gives us hope, reassuring our hearts that when we have stepped away from holiness *we can repent, get sprinkled again with blood, crawl back up on the highway, and be restored to communion with our beloved Savior.*

To remain in holiness *is* a war. We know the war is real, and we're sober about it because the stakes are so high. Our guard is up, and we're determined to stand! If we should ever fall, however, to distraction or discouragement or temptation, we know from David's example that we serve a God who loves to restore. Therefore, we will not be disillusioned. We will not turn away. We shall rise again. We may have lost a battle but we will win this war! His grace and blood are sufficient to renew us to His loving embrace.

Here's what we're going to do: Repent quickly, get sprinkled, get back in His arms, and *stay there.*

Chapter **10**

RIGHTEOUSNESS: PEARL *of* GREAT PRICE

We have talked about drawing near to the Holiest, but I have not yet identified, in a clear and precise way, exactly what qualifies us to approach God. So let's back up a bit and examine our basis for access to the presence of a holy God. It all comes down to one fundamentally necessary commodity.

There is one commodity in the universe that is to be coveted above and beyond all else, and it is this: *Righteousness*. Righteousness is the quality of being just before God, without sin or any defilement. More than anything else, when you stand before God you want to be viewed as righteous in His sight.

Why? Because entrance into God's presence and kingdom is granted only to those who are completely righteous before Him. If you do not meet the full requirements of God's righteousness, He cannot receive you into heaven. His kingdom and presence are too glorious to be sullied by anything that defiles. Any kind of defilement, be it ever so minuscule, disqualifies us from entrance into the eternal city. To gain the high ground of heaven, we must fully meet God's standards of righteousness.

The Bible uses the phrase, "'the wisdom of the just'" (Luke 1:17). Said another way, *righteousness is smart*. You will never do anything wiser than pursue biblical righteousness.

Paul was emphatic in declaring how important this righteousness was to him. It was so important to him that it became the primary pursuit of his life:

> But what things were gain to me, these I have counted loss for Christ. Yet indeed I also count all things loss for the excellence of the knowledge of Christ Jesus my Lord, for whom I have suffered the loss of all things, and count them as rubbish, that I may gain Christ and be found in Him, *not having my own righteousness, which is from the law, but that which is through faith in Christ, the righteousness which is from God by faith*; that I may know Him and the power of His resurrection, and the fellowship of His sufferings, being conformed to His death, if, by any means, I may attain to the resurrection from the dead (Philippians 3:7-11).

Paul wanted, above all, to attain to the resurrection from the dead. And he knew it could happen only by being found in the righteousness of Christ. The best attempts of a human at perfection—even those of an eminent apostle like Paul—were woefully inadequate to satisfy God's righteous requirements.

RIGHTEOUSNESS IS SMART.

When Paul spoke above of a righteousness based on "the law," he meant a righteousness rooted in "performance," because in order to attain the righteousness of the law one had to perform its every edict, down to the last letter. When you see the word "law," therefore, substitute the word "performance" for a clearer meaning. So we could paraphrase Paul to say, "Not having my own righteousness, which is from performance." *Human righteousness is based upon performance.* The only way we can attain righteousness in our own human strength is by meeting every demand of God's law without the slightest shortfall. One tiny mishap and we're consigned to separation from God. "Disqualified!" "Unsatisfactory!" "Imperfect!"

Paul knew that if his admittance into the kingdom was based on his personal performance record, his case was hopeless. He could never perform, in his own strength, to make the cut. *His only hope was to appear before God in the righteousness of Christ.* This is what the gospel has gloriously provided for us. It has made a way for us to appear before God in the very righteousness of Jesus Christ by faith. When I stand before God in the righteousness of Christ, I not only meet God's minimal requirements for admittance into heaven; I also become the recipient of the Father's lavish affections and bountiful riches. Paul was saying, "I do everything I do because I am after just one thing: the righteousness which is from God by faith."

Righteousness is not an end in itself; it is a means to an end. The end is holiness; the means is righteousness. Paul wanted to be in the embrace of the Father, burning in His immediate presence with holiness and light. But to get there required righteousness. Paul was willing to do "whatever it takes" to attain to this righteousness.

Little wonder Paul wrote to Timothy, "Pursue righteousness" (1 Timothy 6:11). This was Paul's top priority and he wanted his spiritual son, Timothy, to catch his values. Jesus admonished His disciples likewise when He told them, "'But seek first the kingdom of God and His righteousness'" (Matthew 6:33).

Seek righteousness! Nothing could be more valuable to your eternal destiny.

Paul Attained His Goal

At the end of his life, when he wrote his final epistle, Paul testified that he had attained to this righteousness.

> I have fought the good fight, I have finished the race, I *have kept the faith*. Finally, *there is laid up for me the crown of righteousness*, which the Lord, the righteous Judge, will give to me on that Day, and not to me only but also to all who have loved His appearing (2 Timothy 4:7-8).

Paul was saying, "I've made it! I've labored all my life to be found in Christ and to stand in the righteousness that comes from faith. Now, at the end of my life, I testify that I have finished this race. The crown of righteousness is mine. I will be dying in a short time, and my Savior is waiting to crown me with the gift of righteousness. It's everything I've ever lived for, and now I know it's mine."

THE RIGHTEOUSNESS OF GOD IS ATTAINED BY FAITH, AND BY FAITH ALONE.

What a glorious, triumphant testimonial to a race well run!

How Is Righteousness Attained?

Someone might ask, "Paul, how did you do it? You were willing to do whatever it took, if, by any means, you might attain to this righteousness. What was your secret?"

Paul's answer was very clear: Faith. "...the righteousness which is from God by faith" (Philippians 3:9).

The righteousness of God is attained by faith, and by faith alone. No man can perform his way (through behavior modification) into this righteousness. The only way to attain the righteousness of Christ is to believe—to believe in His cross, in what His shed blood accomplished, and in His resurrection from the dead. His shed blood purchased the provisions of redemption; His resurrection released those provisions to our planet. When we believe, God accounts it to us as righteousness. Faith! Faith in the blood! It's the only way to righteousness. The priest in the Old Covenant never inspected the offerer; he only inspected the lamb. When the lamb was accepted, the person was accepted. Similarly, under the New Covenant, the sacrifice of the Lamb of God was accepted by God. Now, when you place your faith in His blood, you are accepted (righteous) to God.

sprinkling ➤ righteousness

Faith in the blood brings us into righteousness. Righteousness qualifies us to step into holiness. And holiness is the final end toward which every human heart yearns. Holiness is that place where we burn with fiery affections in the immediate presence of the eternally holy God. It's the ultimate privilege for a human being to experience, and it is granted only to those who stand before God in the righteousness of Christ, by faith.

Faith Produces Righteousness

Faith moves the heart of God in a fascinating way. Said another way, God has a thing for faith. We don't fully understand why He likes it so much; but we do know that it delights and moves His heart in a singularly uncommon way.

Faith is the catalyst for one of the most fascinating transactions in all of Scripture. The transaction is simply this: If you demonstrate faith toward God, God credits you with righteousness. I can't altogether tell you *why* God gives you His righteousness in exchange for your faith; all I know is, that's how God does the math. When you exercise faith in who He is, what He has said, and what He has done, His heart is so moved that He responds by declaring you righteous in His sight.

Hebrews 11 (affectionately known as "the faith chapter") repeatedly emphasizes that faith produces righteousness.

> *By faith Abel* offered to God a more excellent sacrifice than Cain, *through which he obtained witness that he was righteous*, God testifying of his gifts; and through it he being dead still speaks (Hebrews 11:4).

If you were to pop a quiz on some folks and ask them who was the first person in the Bible whose faith God accounted as righteousness, most Christians would answer, "Abraham." But the right answer would be, "Abel." Hebrews 11:4 clearly declares that God saw Abel's faith when he offered his sacrifice and as a result declared Abel to be righteous.

"Well, wasn't Abraham number two on the list?" Nope. The number two slot goes to Noah.

> *By faith Noah*, being divinely warned of things not yet seen, moved with godly fear, prepared an ark for the saving of his household, by which he condemned the world and *became heir of the righteousness which is according to faith* (Hebrews 11:7).

The verse couldn't say it more clearly. Noah inherited righteousness because of his faith.

"Well, was Abraham number three on the list?" Yes, you got it right this time. Abraham was the third man in the Bible to whom God ascribed righteousness because of his faith. "And he believed in the LORD, and He accounted it to him for righteousness" (Genesis 15:6).

What is the source of righteousness? I want you to be real clear about the answer to that question. Do we become righteous by living a blameless lifestyle? No—that's the righteousness of the law, and it's unattainable. There is only one source of true righteousness: Faith. When you place your faith in the gospel of Jesus Christ, righteousness is immediately credited to you. It's simply the way God has chosen to post the transaction.

Sprinkling Makes You Righteous

We get sprinkled with blood for one fundamental reason: Righteousness. The one who gets sprinkled with blood is demonstrating his longing for righteousness. The following Scriptures reveal how Christ's blood makes us righteous (just) in the sight of God.

> In Him we have redemption through His blood, the forgiveness of sins (Ephesians 1:7).

> Much more then, having now been justified by His blood, we shall be saved from wrath through Him (Romans 5:9).

> Therefore Jesus also, that He might sanctify the people with His own blood, suffered outside the gate (Hebrews 13:12).

> And the blood of Jesus Christ His Son cleanses us from all sin (1 John 1:7).

When you ask Jesus to sprinkle you with His blood, that very request is a declaration of faith in what Christ's blood accomplished. When God sees that kind of faith, He immediately answers it by sprinkling you with blood and declaring you righteous in His sight. God accounts your faith in the blood for righteousness.

Faith in the blood says to God:

❖ "I believe Jesus lived a sinless, perfect life. When He died He shed innocent blood."

❖ "I believe He died vicariously for me, that is, He took my place in bearing the punishment for my sin."

❖ "I believe that Christ's blood sprinkled on my life makes me righteous in the sight of God."

sprinkling ➡ righteousness ➡ draw near

When you believe like that in the blood, the next logical step is a no-brainer: Draw near with boldness to the throne of grace, and enjoy the access you have to the affections of God's heart!

The *Work* Of The Cross

To get broken, twisted, sin-ridden human beings into the arms of a holy God is a massive endeavor. Such an endeavor demands enormous labor and Herculean effort. It can happen through works alone, i.e., through very hard work.

"Wait a minute!" I hear someone arguing. "You just finished saying we approach God by *faith*. Now you're saying we approach Him through *works*?"

Yes. But the work required to get a sinner into the presence of a holy God is so gargantuan that no human effort can achieve it. That's why we needed a Champion to come along and do for us what we could not do for ourselves. Only the ultimate Champion, Jesus Christ, could accomplish the required work.

By dying vicariously on the cross, Jesus Christ accomplished what no one else could pull off. He took on the task of making a way for us to draw near to God, and

He didn't relent until it was finished. His blood is now the principal symbol of the work He accomplished. When the Father sees His blood upon our lives, He renders a verdict on our acceptability. "Paid in full! This is the admittance fee into My presence. It was paid by My Son. You have believed in the work of My Son, so now I receive you into My arms."

> TO GET BROKEN, TWIST-ED, SIN-RIDDEN HUMAN BEINGS INTO THE ARMS OF A HOLY GOD IS A MASSIVE ENDEAVOR.

You can get into Father's arms only through works. But there's only one work that satisfies the heart of God: the work of Calvary. Any other effort to get man into God's heart is rejected as woefully inadequate and utterly unacceptable. In fact, *any other work actually angers God because it both rejects the work of God and presumes to suppose that human effort can pull it off.*

The only work God requires of man is this: to *believe* in the work of His Son (John 6:29). When you place your faith in Christ's performance on the cross, all that He accomplished is credited to your account, and you are completely embraced by God.

Faith in Christ's work is your only hope—your only basis—for intimacy with God.

The person who believes in Christ is basically saying to the Father, "I wanted to be near You. But none of my efforts were successful. When I heard what Jesus did for me, it was such good news! I believe without reservation in what Jesus did to get me into Your arms. I have demonstrated that faith by receiving the sprinkling of His blood upon my life. And now here I am, Abba, standing in the righteousness of Christ, and locked in Your embrace. I love You!"

Righteousness Is Not The Same Thing As Holiness

It's important that we understand the difference between righteousness and holiness.

Sprinkling with blood doesn't give you holiness; it gives you righteousness, by faith. Righteousness gives you the *right* to approach God. Then, as you draw near to God, you will enter into holiness.

Righteousness qualifies us for holiness. But to enter into holiness, we must intentionally step forward into the heart of God—and *stay there*.

Here's how I would chart the distinction between righteousness and holiness:

sprinkling ➡ righteousness ➡ draw near ➡ holiness

Sprinkling of blood makes us righteous; righteousness qualifies us to draw near; drawing near brings us into holiness.

"Righteous" refers to our legal status before God; "holy" refers to our location in the heart of God. *Jesus died that we might be blameless in righteousness and burning in holiness.*

To visualize the difference between righteousness and holiness, imagine a wood burning stove. See the walls of the stove as representing righteousness, and the coals inside the stove depicting the flames of holiness. When the walls of righteousness are secure, then it's possible to light the fires of holiness. Without the walls in place, you'll not be able to stoke a fire.

RIGHTEOUSNESS GIVES YOU THE *RIGHT* TO APPROACH GOD.

Keep that picture in mind as you read Jesus' words, "'And because lawlessness will abound, the love of many will grow cold'" (Matthew 24:12). When lawlessness abounds, it means the walls of righteousness have been removed. What is the result? The flame of love goes out and the fire grows cold.

Sometimes the walls of righteousness can make us feel hemmed in, but in this case it's a constriction that is for our good. The walls of a stove are designed to "hem in" the burning coals. The closer the walls of righteousness are drawn in, the hotter the furnace of holiness can burn.

While some things may seem "permissible" to the saint, not all things are automatically "beneficial" (1 Corinthians 10:23). Anything that widens or loosens our walls of righteousness is not our friend, if it causes the fires of holiness to cool.

The one who is seeking true holiness actually desires for the lines of righteousness to be drawn in and become even more confining, because the more hemmed in we are by the walls of righteousness, the hotter the fires of holiness can burn.

Changed Behavior

One of the main benefits of holiness is changed behavior. As we abide in the holy place, God changes our very DNA and conforms us to the image of Christ. The Bible word for changed behavior is "sanctification."

I said earlier that the end of the Christian life is holiness. Because when we attain to holiness, we are abiding in the procreative womb of divine life where anything and everything becomes possible. *It's here, in the womb of holiness, that God dramatically changes our behavior and attitudes, until we shine with the very radiance of Christ.*

The longing of the believer is to be so transformed that we become godly and blameless in every facet of our lifestyles. We will not attain those changes, however, by focusing on our behavior; rather, we will be changed as

we draw near to God in holiness and focus on His counte-
nance. As we behold Him, He changes us.

sprinkling ➞ righteousness ➞ draw near ➞
holiness ➞ changed behavior

Now our chart is complete. Sprinkling of blood makes
us righteous; righteousness qualifies us to draw near; drawing near brings us into holiness; and holiness is the place
where our behavior is actually transformed by the power
of God and our willing cooperation with His grace.

Perhaps the best way I can explain how holiness leads
to sanctification (changed behavior) is by illustrating with
a story. The following story is from my assistant, Hollie,
which she shared with me just this morning.

After Hollie became a Christian, she was made righteous by the blood of Christ, but she still continued to
cuss. She was active in church and Bible studies, but her
tongue still reflected her former life. Then, when some
of her friends decided to go on a 21-day fast, she joined
them. She drew close to God in a new way during that
fast. About 17 days into the fast she realized, she hadn't
cussed in 17 days! Drawing near to God had produced a
change in her behavior that she wasn't even expecting or
asking for.

Hollie was legally righteous the day she believed in
Christ and the cross. That righteousness qualified her to
step into holiness. When she stepped into holiness in an
intentional way during her 21-day fast, God's holiness
changed her at an accelerated rate. The power of that
place of consecration brought her into a new level of victory in her practical everyday life. In other words, holiness
changed her behavior.

Here's the secret of the Christian life: Get sprinkled

with blood, enter into the presence of God with boldness, burn in holiness, and then watch Him change you!

Now let me tell you the heights to which changed thoughts, attitudes, and behavior can take you.

Chapter 11

SPRINKLED *in* INNOCENCE

As a redeemed child of God, you have the glorious privilege of being cleansed by the blood of Christ from every defiling sin and standing with complete confidence before Him. You can come to Him at any time, ask to be sprinkled with blood, and be renewed in righteousness and holiness before Him. Any time your conscience strikes you, you have a way through the blood to be immediately renewed and cleansed. It's glorious!

But there's something even more glorious.

It's the glory of being sprinkled with blood when your conscience *isn't* striking you and when you're aware of *no known sin.*

It's awesome to know you can receive the cleansing of Christ's blood when you feel the need to be washed. It's even more awesome, though, to receive the sprinkling of blood when you have no awareness of sin or defilement.

In this instance, you're getting sprinkled with blood—not because of sin issues in your life, for your conscience is clear. You're getting sprinkled with blood—not because you want to draw near to God, for you're already in His embrace. You're getting sprinkled with blood—not because you want to be made holy, for you're already standing in the holy place.

Why get sprinkled in blood, then, if you need none of those provisions?

You're getting sprinkled with blood—simply because you cherish the sacrifice of Calvary, your heart is overflowing in love for your Bridegroom, and you're celebrating with gratefulness the nobility of your high calling in God.

Washing In Innocence

Here's how David talked about it:

> I will wash my hands in innocence; so I will
> go about Your altar, O Lord (Psalm 26:6).

David was saying, "Lord, I am walking in innocence before You. I know of nothing that is against me. But even though my conscience is clear, I still want to be washed and cleansed by Your blood—because I know I don't stand before You on the merit of a clean conscience. I stand before You on the merit of Your cleansing power in my life. As You are now washing me again, You are giving me boldness to walk all around Your altar and minister to You."

When you're aware of defilement in your life, getting sprinkled with blood grants you great boldness to draw near to God without reservation. However, when you are walking in innocence before God, and *then* you get sprinkled, it grants an even *greater* confidence. It's the confidence that comes in knowing that God's grace is producing long-term change in you. You truly are learning to perfect holiness in the fear of the Lord. You are no longer hounded with pockets of cyclical failure and habitual sin. Your righteousness is no longer merely a technical status with God; even better, you've found the reality of living in *innocence*.

Living in innocence and sprinkled with blood— BOOM, you're doubly dangerous! This is where you begin to truly taste of the reality of Proverbs 28:1, "The righteous are bold as a lion." Getting sprinkled in innocence gives you "confidence squared."

Now you have the confidence to go all about the altar of God, ministering to Him, serving Him, worshiping Him, blessing Him. The courts of the King have now become your habitual stomping grounds. You're at home in the midst of the fiery stones, serving at the altar of the High Priest of Heaven. This kind of confidence makes you bold with strength in your soul.

Getting Past Self-Awareness

One of the benefits of innocence is that we cease to be hounded with thoughts of inadequacy and unworthiness before God. And when you're gazing on God, the last thing you want is to be distracted with sheepish feelings of unworthiness. All you want, in that moment, is to be engulfed in His glory and consumed with fascination at His beauty.

Perhaps I can make my meaning clearer by pointing to some of the men in the Bible who had unusually powerful encounters with God. There's a few Bible men whose eyes were opened and they saw God. One of the common elements in their encounters, however, was their sudden awareness of their own depravity and vileness. This overwhelming feeling of self-inadequacy, when standing before God, was articulated by:

❖ Job: Here are Job's famous words when he finally saw God. "'I have heard of You by the hearing of the ear, but now my eye sees You. Therefore I abhor myself, and repent in dust and ashes'" (Job 42:5-6).

❖ Isaiah: When Isaiah was caught up to the throne of God, the first words out of his mouth were, "'Woe is me, for I am undone! Because I am a man of unclean lips, and I dwell in the midst of a people of unclean lips; for my eyes have seen the King, the LORD of hosts'" (Isaiah 6:5).

❖ Peter: When Peter saw the glory of Jesus in the way He supernaturally provided for a huge catch of fish, he exclaimed, "'Depart from me, for I am a sinful man, O Lord!'" (Luke 5:8).

❖ John: When John saw Jesus among the lampstands, here's how it affected him. "And when I saw Him, I fell at His feet as dead" (Revelation 1:17).

❖ Daniel: Daniel had a variety of reactions to the glory of God. After one encounter he was sick for days (Daniel 8:27). On another occasion, he trembled on his hands and knees (Daniel 10:10).

The point is: Common to their experience, when confronted with the glory and holiness of the Lord, was this sudden awareness of their personal sinfulness and spiritual bankruptcy.

GOD IS LEADING US ON A PATH WHERE WE EVENTUALLY LOSE THE PAINFUL AWARENESS OF OUR INADEQUACIES.

However, God is leading us on a path where we eventually lose the painful awareness of our inadequacies. In the end, we will stand face to face with Christ and have none of the feelings of inferiority that come from battling with sin issues. What confidence and joy we will have in that hour, when He has presented us to Himself faultless and with great glory!

David pointed to this attainment of grace when he wrote,

As for me, I will see Your face in righteousness; I shall be satisfied when I awake in Your likeness (Psalm 17:15).

O to see His face in righteousness! There is a day coming when we will be so confident in our robes of righteousness that we will gaze upon the face of Christ and not be distracted by feelings of inadequacy. Instead, we will be "satisfied" with the thrill of beholding His glory for we will awaken in His likeness.

The goal is not to lose all self-awareness when standing before God; rather, the goal is to lose all awareness of *sinfulness*.

There is a kind of self-awareness that actually enhances the worship experience. We see it illustrated in the worship of the living creatures around the throne.

The Living Creatures Are Properly Self-Aware

The four living creatures who serve before the throne of God never cease to worship, for "they do not rest day or night, saying: 'Holy, holy, holy, Lord God Almighty, who was and is and is to come!'" (Revelation 4:8). When John saw them, he described them as "full of eyes *around* and *within*" (Revelation 4:8). The original word for "within" means, "from inside," or, "inwardly." When they worship, the living creatures look "around" and also "within." Thus, worship in its fullness looks both around and within.

They look around: The living creatures are preoccupied with gazing upon God, and while worshiping Him they are also looking around at others in the worship gathering.

They look within: While worshiping, the living creatures are also looking inside at their own emotions.

Worship that is fully formed, therefore, looks in three

directions: at God, at other worshipers, and within. Their many eyes indicate that they look in all three directions *simultaneously*.

Worship is first and foremost a preoccupation with God—gazing, peering, listening, watching, absorbing, searching, admiring, extolling, identifying, gaping, thrilling. And while we never take our eyes off God, we broaden our perspective to enjoy the group dynamics of those nearby. As we behold their exuberance, abandonment, fervency, and the glory that rests upon them, our worship is further enhanced. Ezekiel saw torches of fire being exchanged between these creatures (Ezekiel 1:13), which reflected how they fueled each other's worship. In a similar way, *we ignite one another in corporate worship*. We enjoy each other while enjoying God.

WE ENJOY EACH OTHER WHILE ENJOYING GOD.

But worship also looks within. I am not speaking of a self-absorption that distracts us from God, or feelings of inadequacy that deflate our ability to worship, but an awareness that beholding God is delightful and pleasurable. Let me illustrate from the example of a young couple that is courting.

When a young couple spends time together, they're evaluating their relationship based upon how much they enjoy each other. After an evening together, the young woman might turn to her escort and say, "Thanks for tonight, I enjoyed myself." She is conveying, "Being in your presence is fun. Your company delights me. I like who I am when I'm with you." While her primary focus was on *him* during the evening, her self-awareness made her evening complete.

In a similar way, the divine romance finds its fulfillment when both parties enjoy themselves in the presence of each other.

When we stand before God, our primary focus is upon who He is—His glory, power, majesty, and beauty. Our secondary focus is upon how we and others around us are experiencing feelings of delight and wonder in the presence of such majestic glory. It's certainly not our first thought—but it does occur to us, "I'm really enjoying being with You, Lord!"

While the fullness of this kind of delight and confidence is reserved for the age to come, God's grace has provided for us to experience *significant* levels of exhilaration in our intimacy with God even now. We have an invitation before us, to search out what dimensions of grace and glory the Lord will release to the human spirit in this present age.

Here's what we're after. We want to get sprinkled with blood, be made confident in righteousness, and draw near to holiness with no awareness of personal inadequacy. No shame, no self-consciousness. Total confidence in love!

When we know we succumbed to temptation a few hours back, it's difficult to draw near to God without any sense of personal inadequacy. Negative feelings of self-awareness can steal the joy of intimacy out of our hearts. This is why we want God's holiness to empower us toward changed behavior. We're in pursuit of this attainment David called "innocence." When we are walking in innocence, it means we are not aware of personal compromise. When we get sprinkled in this place of innocence, all awareness of inadequacy melts away, and we gain amazing confidence to stand before God and go all about His altar.

THE DIVINE ROMANCE FINDS ITS FULFILLMENT WHEN BOTH PARTIES ENJOY THEMSELVES IN THE PRESENCE OF EACH OTHER.

Any inner conflict that causes us to feel shame or

unworthiness in the presence of God is to be targeted as undesirable. *The sprinkling of blood cleanses our guilty conscience; then the passionate pursuit of innocence further strengthens our boldness before God.*

An Everlasting Witness

Before closing this chapter, I want to point out a fascinating characteristic of the sprinkling of blood. There's something about it that goes beyond just our need to receive, in this life, cleansing from an evil conscience. There is something about it that will be eternally relevant to us, even in our glorified state. I hardly know how to speak of it, but let me try.

When Cain killed his brother Abel, the blood of Abel called out from the ground, "Vengeance! Get justice for me because my life was taken from me in innocence."

Jesus' blood also cries out from the ground in Jerusalem, where it was shed. But Jesus' blood doesn't cry for retribution; rather, His blood calls out, "Forgive them! Receive them! Accept them, Abba, into Your arms!"

This is why the writer of Hebrews gave us this marvelous passage:

> But you have come to Mount Zion and to the city of the living God, the heavenly Jerusalem, to an innumerable company of angels, to the general assembly and church of the firstborn who are registered in heaven, to God the Judge of all, to the spirits of just men made perfect, to Jesus the Mediator of the new covenant, and to the blood of sprinkling that speaks better things than that of Abel (Hebrews 12:22-24).

I want you to notice something about this passage. Every phrase in it describes *eternal* realities, i.e., characteristics of Christ's kingdom that will be true for all eternity.

❖ Mount Zion (the city of the living God, the heavenly Jerusalem) will be our home *forever.*

❖ We will live in the company of angels *forever.*

❖ We will be part of the general assembly (the church of the firstborn) *forever.*

❖ We will be in the presence of God the Judge *forever.*

❖ The spirits of just men will be made perfect *forever.*

❖ Jesus will be our Mediator of the new covenant *forever.*

Since all those kingdom characteristics are *eternal* in their relevance and scope, it follows that the last item in the list (which I haven't mentioned yet) is also an eternal reality. Here it is:

❖ The blood of sprinkling will be upon our lives *forever.*

Think about it: We will get sprinkled with blood *forever.* Even after sin and death have been destroyed, and we are dwelling with God in sinless perfection, we will *still* enjoy the privilege of being sprinkled with blood.

EVEN AFTER SIN AND DEATH HAVE BEEN DESTROYED, AND WE ARE DWELLING WITH GOD IN SINLESS PERFECTION, WE WILL STILL ENJOY THE PRIVILEGE OF BEING SPRINKLED WITH BLOOD.

We won't get sprinkled with blood in order to be cleansed from sin, for there will be no sin in the eternal city. Why, then, will we get sprinkled with blood when we are living in such glorious innocence? Here's why: We'll gratefully bathe in His sprinkled blood as an act of reverence and worship, to commemorate and venerate the Lamb of God in whose riven breast we have found our eternal repose.

This privilege the angels will never share. They are never sprinkled with the blood of Christ. Christ's blood is for redeemed humans only.

Peter reminded us that the blood of Christ is not corruptible like gold or silver (1 Peter 1:18). It is eternal—eternally available, eternally efficacious, and eternally fresh.

For all eternity, we will revel in the rich salvation Christ provided for us at Calvary. In the ages to come, we will demonstrate our loyalty to the blood of Christ by receiving His sprinkling upon our hearts. We will enjoy, forever, the fellowship of saints who have been made perfect, and who will ever dignify the sacrifice of the cross by receiving the sprinkling of blood upon their lives.

The blood of sprinkling is so important, and so holy, it will be ours to enjoy *forever*.

Chapter 12

MY BASEBALL STORY

I'd like to tell a personal story that underscored for me the privilege and power of choosing to live in the bosom of the Father.

The summer of 1994 was one of the darkest seasons of my entire life. I'll explain.

As mentioned earlier, I suffered a vocal injury in 1992. After a bad surgery, my voice became very weak and very sore to use. Being a pastor and worship leader at the time, I could read the handwriting on the wall. What does a pastor do who can't talk? What does a worship leader do who can't sing? Unless something changed, it was becoming increasingly clear that I would not be able to continue pastoring the church we loved.

I was in pain in almost every compartment of life.

❖ I was in professional pain—I was called, trained, and ordained to minister the word of God and to lead God's people, but that appeared to be coming to an end.

❖ I was in physical pain—I would use my voice each day until the pain took over and I simply had to stop because my throat was raw.

✤ I was in theological pain—I didn't have a verse for what had happened to me. Understanding in the Scriptures was to come eventually, but in the first couple years I was flailing frantically to stay afloat theologically. "God, do You do this kind of stuff to Your friends? And if You do...who *are* You, anyways?"

✤ I was in relational pain—relationships are maintained through communication, and suddenly I found myself physically incapable of nurturing the relationships I valued. Many of my friendships slowly began to drift into the distance while I watched, helpless to do anything about it.

✤ I was in emotional/mental pain—for the first time in my life I was wrestling with the hellish beast of depression. The disability was changing my personality in ways I didn't even like. Previous to the injury I always had an optimistic, even-keeled, cheerful disposition. Suddenly, my ability to envision future possibilities was decimated. Every visionary idea that ever came to mind required a voice to implement. A hopeful future had suddenly turned into a hopeless prospect of interminable pain.

When I lost my voice, trying to pastor a church became exceedingly distressful to me. I can remember mixing with my flock on Sunday mornings, carrying a notepad with me, and writing out to people, "How are you doing?" Or writing to a new family, "Thanks for coming, where are you from?" For the record, it's virtually impossible to pastor people while writing to them on a notepad. My heart ached to wrap my arms around them and express my affection and care, but I was physically incapable of expressing myself.

The pain of trying to still pastor with no voice was

intense, but there were two areas that were even more painful for me. The first related to my children. While the limited ability to communicate with my wife, Marci, was very painful for me, the struggle to connect verbally with my children was even harder. One reason was because I would give what little voice I might have on a particular day to my wife first, and the kids would have to settle for whatever was left (which was often nothing). Another reason was because communicating on a notepad was possible with my wife, but really quite impractical in relating to my kids. So the loss of vocal interaction with my kids was especially tough for me.

It was my custom before the injury to coach my children in Bible memorization while feeding them breakfast. Between bites, we would see who could recite the verses best. Then we'd stop for prayer. Then hugs. And finally, they'd run off to the school bus.

At bedtime, I told them Bible stories, and often we would act them out in our living room. Neighborhood children would sometimes join us for these animated interactions with the great stories of the Bible. We would kneel together at the sofa and pray. After being tucked into bed, they were never satisfied until we laid hands on them and prayed one final blessing. This was altogether my joy and delight.

When my voice took the hit, everything changed. My wife was able to continue to train them spiritually, but for myself, I was simply incapable of continuing with Bible memorization, Bible stories, and family prayers. I could still lay hands on them, but my prayers were mostly silent. The priority of training up my children in the way they should go was paramount to me, and now my inability to fulfill this role in their lives in the way I desired was more painful to me than words can express.

Almost equal to that, in terms of personal emotional distress, was my inability to sing any longer. Singing was my primary vehicle for expressing love and praise and worship to God. It was my daily practice to sing from the word in my personal times with God in the morning. I would often sit down spontaneously at the piano when I might have a couple spare moments, and such times almost always meant singing while I played. I sang when I led worship from the keyboard. I was not a good singer—I mean, I didn't have a solo-quality voice—but I loved to worship my Lord and singing was almost always a part of that. Something happens within the soul when you fill your lungs with air and let out a sound of praise to the One you love. The release that attends singing is revitalizing to the soul. But for me, suddenly, all that was gone. It hurt too much to attempt to sing. When the song dried up, so did my joy in playing the keyboard. For me, singing and playing went hand in hand; so when I could no longer sing, I seemed to lose any reason to play the piano. My song died. It was such an intrinsic part of my life, and when it died, the grief that swept my soul—well, I don't know how to put it into words.

I share these things to give you a little peek into my emotional chemistry in 1994. Not only had the losses in these areas overwhelmed my soul, but there was no prognosis for my vocal status to improve—until God should step in supernaturally, perform His word, and heal me. Divine healing became, and still is, the only hope of release from this prison. But when would the healing come? If the release of healing will come sometime in the future, then how do I process my pain over my inability to share with my children today?

Word Immersion

For the first time in my life, I was tasting of suffering. Entire sections of Scripture that had previously been meaningless to me were suddenly incredibly relevant. I identified with Job when he wrote, "'Therefore I am terrified at His presence; when I consider this, I am afraid of Him. For God made my heart weak, and the Almighty terrifies me; because I was not cut off from the presence of darkness, and He did not hide deep darkness from my face'" (Job 23:15-17).

> RHEMA IS WHAT HAPPENS WHEN GOD SPEAKS A WORD TO ME; LOGOS IS WHAT HAPPENS WHEN I TELL THAT WORD TO YOU.

I never had a depressed day in my life until the vocal injury. Now, I found myself in hand-to-hand combat with depression on almost a constant basis. When oppressed and depressed, I found but one thing to help me in the fight to stay in faith: God's word. The Bible is an astounding book. It speaks life, light, and hope into the darkest of circumstances. I began to fall in love with God's word all over again. Whenever the Lord would give me a *rhema* word, it always broke a hole in the clouds of oppression and lifted my spirit with renewed confidence in God's good plans for my life.

Let me explain my term, "*rhema* word." There are two Greek words in the original language of the New Testament manuscripts that are translated by the English word, "word." Those two Greek words are *logos* and *rhema*.

Here's how I distinguish between them: *Rhema* is what happens when God speaks a word to me; *logos* is what happens when I tell that word to you. A *rhema* is a word spoken directly from God to a person's heart. When you repeat to someone else a *rhema* that God gave you, it doesn't come to the other person as a *rhema*, it's downgraded to a *logos*. You can't give a *rhema* to someone else; only heaven can.

The Bible is rightly called the *logos* of God. When the words of the Bible were initially conveyed to the Bible's authors, they came to them as a *rhema* word. But when they wrote them down, those words become *logos*.

The power of God's word is in the *rhema* word, because when you get a *rhema*, it's a living word that proceeds from the mouth of God. *Rhema* is addressed directly to your heart and life, and it explodes within your mind and heart with divine revelation, insight, and potency. The most common way you receive a *rhema* from God is by immersing yourself in the *logos* (the written word of God). As you spend hours of loving meditation in God's word, you are setting yourself up to receive a *rhema*. Stay with it long enough and you'll eventually receive one. It's guaranteed. The Bible has promised that if you sow to the Spirit, you will reap of the Spirit (Galatians 6:8). So if you will sow chunks of time into meditating in the *logos*, one of these days you'll get a *rhema*.

I live my life by this assurance. This is why I spend time in God's word. I'm desperate to receive a *rhema*— a living word directly to my heart that feeds, nourishes, strengthens, empowers, and renews my mind in the truth of God's ways.

Back to my story. When I lost my voice, I found myself fighting an incessant battle with discouragement and depression. I knew only one thing to do in that fight, and that was to spend as much time as possible in the word (*logos*). Because the only thing that would break through the oppression was a *rhema* word from God, and the only way I knew to get a *rhema* was by word-immersion in the *logos*.

The Summer Of 1994

As the spring of 1994 approached, I grew increasingly desperate regarding my vocal situation. It was almost two years since the initial injury, and my condition had progressively deteriorated. My volume levels had plummeted while the pain levels had soared. I was still pastoring our church, but I was doing the math and knew that unless something changed I would eventually have to resign the pastorate.

In the spring of 1994, I embarked on my most desperate measure up to that point. I went on a 21-day water fast, in solitude. When I went into it, I told my wife, "I'm going to fast for 21 days, then I'm coming home to resign the ministry. It's over."

As I immersed myself in the word during those 21 days, I focused my greatest energy on the Gospels. Suddenly, I found myself being hit with *rhema* after *rhema*. It was perhaps the most life-changing experience I'd ever had. The Lord fed me powerfully from His word and met me in a strong way.

The feeding of that prayer retreat sustained me for a couple months. But there was no change in my vocal status, and I continued to be greatly distressed by the physical disability. In June I said to the church elders, "I can't go on. But neither can I resign. The Lord won't let me resign. I don't know what to do. I can't continue and I can't quit."

The church elders prayerfully considered with me what to do. The answer, it seemed, was for me to take a sabbatical. They graciously released me to take a sabbatical for a maximum of six months. The church paid my full salary during that time, and I devoted myself entirely to the word and prayer. So during the summer of 1994, I was on a paid sabbatical.

"Wow!" you may be thinking, "How awesome is that!? Six months on full salary, with nothing to do but enjoy the summer." Truth be told, it was agonizingly awful. I was flailing like a drowning man, gasping for air, trying to stay alive, and wondering how much longer I could possibly survive. I had six months to get hold of God and figure out what was happening with my life. I felt like a man on death row.

The oppression over my soul during that summer was so thick it seemed I could cut it with a knife. It was the worst summer of my life. If I received an insight from the word of God, it felt like a gulp of air to a drowning man. It kept me alive, but death seemed imminent.

The worst part of my week was going to church. Since I was the senior pastor, I felt it was right and necessary to take my family to church each weekend, even though I had zero responsibilities in the services. But dragging myself to church was painful beyond description. Our church was in three weekend services at the time, and we would go to the Saturday night service to get it over with. I can still remember what it felt like to sit in the center section, third row from the front, unable to sing, trying to appear engaged during the praise service when everything inside me wanted to run from the building. I longed to reach out to the flock but was vocally strapped. I could feel the eyes of everyone upon me as I stood in the front, writhing in emotional pain and trying to conceal my struggle. The preeminent question in everyone's mind seemed to be, "What about Bob? What is God doing with Bob?"

Black Sabbath

I remember this one weekend as being particularly dark. It was Saturday, which meant going to church, and I was dreading it. A cloud of oppression lay thick upon my mind, and I was doing my utmost to shake it. I spent several hours that day in prayer and the word, but I couldn't escape the dread of the Saturday evening service that loomed before me.

The thing that comforted me was the thought, "Okay, I'll go to church tonight; but then I'll get up Sunday morning and I won't have to go to church. (Thank God!) I'll get in my reading chair, I'll open my Bible, and I'll soak in the word. Perhaps God will speak something to my heart tomorrow from the word. If He does, I know the clouds will break, a shaft of sunlight will penetrate through to my soul, and I'll be able to live for one more day."

So we went to the Saturday service. I was relieved when it was over. I came home and went straight to bed. Then I got up Sunday morning, settled into my chair with my Bible, and began to implore God for a *rhema*. "Please! Please! Please!"

Nothing.

I tried praying.

Dry as dust.

That went on for two or three hours.

Finally, I literally threw my Bible on the ground, and declared in my soul, "This is it! I've had it! Enough! I'm sick of all this naval-gazing self-pity. Me, me, me. My, my, my. My pain, my little world, my depression. All this preoccupation with my pain levels is nauseating. If I'm going to hurt this much, my kids are going to have a good time today. I'm taking them to a baseball game!"

"IF I'M GOING TO HURT THIS MUCH, MY KIDS ARE GOING TO HAVE A GOOD TIME TODAY."

Now, I was raised in a good Christian home, and in our tradition Christians didn't go to baseball games on Sunday. In fact, Christians rarely went to baseball games period.

So I had never been to a professional or semi-professional baseball game. And I certainly had never been to a sports event on a Sunday! But I was in too much pain to give a hoot about all that. I had made my decision; my kids were going to have fun. I'm taking them to a baseball game.

The Rochester "Red Wings" were the local triple-A ball team and they were playing a home game that day, so I found out what I needed to know to get to the game. I threw my three kids into our minivan, collected a couple neighborhood boys, and took off with the five kids for Silver Stadium in Rochester, New York.

I felt the same way a first-timer to church must feel. "Where do you park?" "Where's the entrance?" "How much is it?" "Where are the restrooms?"

As it turned out, we had stumbled upon a special day at the ballpark. They were giving out free baseball cards to all the kids in attendance. What's more, the players were mingling with the fans and signing cards for the kids. My kids went scurrying for autographs.

"Everybody gets popcorn!" I growled. "Everyone gets a Coke. Everybody gets a hotdog!" I was in an ornery way, and it was to my kids' advantage.

We found our seats. It was an absolutely gorgeous day. Picture perfect. Mid-summer, blue skies, 75 degrees, baseball in America. Does it get better than this? My kids had their hats on, with their baseball gloves in their laps, and they were stuffing their faces. They were having a blast.

THE ACCUSATIONS WERE SCREAMING IN MY EAR, "GOD'S MAD AT YOU. HE HAS REJECTED YOU. YOU'RE A CASUALTY. IT'S OVER."

Me? I was absolutely miserable. The cloud over my soul hadn't budged even a fraction of an inch. I was glad my kids were happy, but I myself was engulfed in depression.

Which Voice To Believe?

I began to talk to myself. "I wonder if God knows where I'm at." I didn't mean, "I wonder if God knows that I'm at a baseball game on a Sunday afternoon." What I meant was, "I wonder if God knows how I'm feeling right now. I'm spending all of my time in the word and prayer—I mean, they're *paying* me to pray right now. And even though I'm coming after God as hard as I know to, I can't shake this oppression over my mind. I have no idea what else to do. Does God see me right now? Is He even aware of my pursuit and my struggle? Does He know about my battles with discouragement? Does He see where I'm at?"

Then my self-talk took another turn. "What have I done? Why is God so angry at me? I must have done something terribly wrong to incur such wrath. I've repented of everything I can think of, but it's probably not enough. Maybe I've done something to anger Him without even knowing it."

The accusations were screaming in my ear, "God's mad at you. He has rejected you. You're a casualty. It's over. You'll never recover. You're beyond repair. You're forsaken of God." All the data at the physical level seemed to corroborate the testimony of those accusations.

But at the same time, a very quiet, almost imperceptible voice was whispering in the other ear, *"I am with you. I have chosen you. I am for you. I have a purpose for your life. This thing is going somewhere. It's not over. I know the plans I have for you, plans to prosper you and not to harm you, to give you a hope and a future."*

The volume of the loud voice was so overwhelming, and the data at the natural level so dreadfully confirming, that I couldn't tell if the quiet voice was real or just my imagination. "Could it be possible that God likes me, that

He is for me, and that instead of forsaking me He is actually choosing me?"

My self-talk took yet another turn. "I wonder if God is with me. I wonder if He understands where I'm at. If He does, I wonder if He'd give me a sign. A sign, to show that He loves me."

As soon as that thought entered my head, I immediately doused it. "Don't go there, Bob! Don't tempt God by asking for a sign! Thou shalt not tempt the Lord thy God!"

There's no way I was going to ask God if He would let me catch a baseball as a sign. Nope. Nada. Nix. "Don't even think like that, Bob. You would be setting yourself up for something *really* bad. Get the idea out of your head. Do not ask God for a baseball!"

Then the thoughts morphed into this question, "I wonder if God would *let* me catch a baseball, to show me that He understands where I'm at, that He loves me, and that He's with me." I wasn't making a request of God; it was just an inner query, "I wonder if God would."

"This is bad thinking," argued my reasonable side. "This kind of thinking is a set-up for massive disappointment. You're depressed enough already. Get it out of your head."

So I pushed it away. But even as I pushed it aside, the question still kept popping up, "I wonder if God would give me a sign."

Doing The Math, Πr^2

While the rational side of my brain kept sweeping the question away, the analytical side of my brain started making math calculations. I couldn't stop my brain. Something inside wanted to know, "I wonder what my odds are of catching a baseball."

Being my first time at a professional-level baseball game, I began to add up the factors that would help me compute my chances. The first question was, "How many balls are being caught by fans?" The answer was, "They're not catching baseballs."

I tried to recall some of my tenth-grade geometry. Take the circumference of the field; multiply that by Πr squared. Divide that by the number of fans present. Divided by the number of balls being caught. I'm doing the math. "Bob, stop this, this is insane. You won't be catching a baseball in this game. Your chances are zero."

Furthermore, we were in a section of bleachers that was shaded by an overhang—there was another level of bleachers over our heads—so a ball wouldn't be able to get all the way to us even if it tried. "Forget it, Bob, you're not going to be getting a baseball today."

I did my best to dismiss the crazy notion.

Pop Fly

We were about three quarters of the way through the game by now. One of the "Americans" was up to bat. He hit a fly ball that headed for the stands. As it approached the stands, with one motion hundreds of fans moved simultaneously to their feet. Gloves appeared out of nowhere. Hands reached to the heavens. And I was on my feet with the rest of the fools.

The ball came up toward our section. It came underneath the overhang, hit one of the crossbeams that supported the flooring over our heads, careened off the crossbeam at a *bizarre* angle, and came flying straight for me. As I cupped my hands to try to stop the ball (it was coming at me with frightening speed), it pushed through my arms, bounced off my chest, and landed squarely in my daughter, Katie's, lap.

I sank into my seat next to her, stunned. "Daddy, I got a baseball!" she said to me, squealing with delight. I didn't have the heart to say it to her, but I was thinking, "That's not *your* baseball, Sweetheart, that's *my* baseball!"

I picked up the baseball and just stared at it. It was real. I was holding a baseball. God had given me a baseball.

An elderly gentleman sitting in front of me said to me, "I've been coming to baseball games here every week for over thirty years, and I've never caught a baseball." That helped give me perspective on the uniqueness of what had just happened.

I'M RESOLVED. I WILL GET SPRINKLED WITH BLOOD EVERY DAY.

Here's my take on it. I understood God to be saying, "I am with you. I love you. I understand where you're at. I love the way you're pursuing Me. Abide in the word. Persevere in prayer. Keep coming after Me with all your heart. I am for you. I have great plans for your life. It's not over. You have a hope and a future."

I call that baseball my "kiss from God." It was a sign from God, in the face of my blackest darkness, of His affection and good designs for my life.

So I'm resolved. I will get sprinkled with blood every day, and come with boldness into the throneroom. I will live in the bosom of the Father, leaning on Jesus' breast. I will abide in the place of holiness. Because I know if I will just stay here, it's impossible for my life to remain unchanged. He finishes the stories of His holy ones. By His grace, I shall not be moved. I will stay here, in His arms, until He perfects that which concerns me. He is a good Father, and He will complete the good work He has started.

Chapter 13

OUR PLEDGE *to* APPROACH GOD

The blood of Jesus is our way into an altogether glorious, intimate, abiding relationship with Abba Father. Jesus died to get us into Abba's arms. His cross says, "I'm willing to pay the ultimate price, if that's what it takes to get you into the Father's bosom, because I know if I can just *get* you there, everything will work out fine from there."

I see His blood, I see the extravagance of the price He paid, and I see the thrilling intimacy He has made available to me. Therefore, God forbid that I should ever neglect this glorious privilege of approaching Him!

Approaching the throne of grace, however, is more than just an awesome privilege. It's a holy responsibility. We have been entrusted with a stewardship: to sit with Christ in heavenly places and, from that place of ruling, bring the Kingdom of God from heaven to earth. We will give account one day for how we stewarded the access to God which Christ's cross granted us.

There is a generation—and I believe it's today's generation—that is willing to come into covenantal loyalty related to the sprinkling of Christ's blood. The blood of Jesus will be so important to them that they will make an inner vow to get sprinkled with Christ's blood daily, and spend every day of their lives in the bosom of the Father.

Making A Pledge

"I make a pledge before heaven to get sprinkled with blood every day, approach God with confidence, and live out the rest of my days in the Holiest."

The Lord has gently nudged me into this pledge. I didn't come into it all in one day. It began by being awakened to the blessing of enjoying instant intimacy with God through the sprinkling of God. The more I did it, the more I realized, "This really works! I'm really there! Even though I can't see it with my physical eyes, I am actually living every day in the embrace of God." My resolve began to grow. "I'm going to do this every day!"

APPROACHING THE THRONE OF GRACE IS A HOLY RESPONSIBILITY.

As I received the sprinkling of blood every day, a confidence grew in my heart that I could really make this my practice all my days. Then, just when I thought my resolve was at its height, the Lord led me to upgrade it to an even greater intensity. He invited me to make a personal pledge before Him. What had been my resolve had now become my vow.

Such a vow is actually scriptural.

> "'Then I will cause him to draw near, and
> he shall approach Me; for who is this who
> pledged his heart to approach Me?' says the
> LORD" (Jeremiah 30:21).

When I saw this verse, I became awestruck. "There's actually a verse for making this kind of a vow!" I reflected to myself.

This verse speaks of the man who will pledge his heart to approach God every day. In its context, it's referring to the governor of Jerusalem in the Millennial Kingdom who will make a personal vow to come to Jesus every day to debrief and receive fresh directives. (Jesus will be physically enthroned in Jerusalem at that time, so the proximity will make that vow feasible.) But the verse also applies to us in a spiritual way. There is a generation today who is unwilling to relegate this kind of consecration only to the Millennium. There are young men and women today who are ready to pledge their hearts to the blood of Christ and promise before God to approach him every day of their lives, step into holiness, and stay there.

When we consider what Christ's blood has provided for us, why should we ever again want to spend a solitary day away from the throneroom of heaven? Burning in the presence of the King has become our portion, our inheritance, and our delight. Our soul refuses to ever again live a day outside His courts.

"Never again a day outside Your embrace, Abba!"

Somebody might wonder, "But how about down time? Aren't we ever allowed to have times of relaxation when we don't have to be 'on' spiritually?"

Moments of leisure or respite spent outside God's presence aren't down time, they're "downer" time. We all need times of recreation and refreshment; however, why should we step out of holiness and use our down time to become defiled and depleted? Rather, let's take advantage of our down time by getting rejuvenated in the wisdom of holiness. Time spent outside the embrace of Abba Father isn't relaxing and therapeutic, it's oppressive and stressful. Authentic rejuvenation happens when recreational activities are pursued while the heart is engaged in communion with God.

> THERE ARE YOUNG MEN AND WOMEN TODAY WHO ARE READY TO PLEDGE THEIR HEARTS TO THE BLOOD OF CHRIST AND PROMISE BEFORE GOD TO APPROACH HIM EVERY DAY OF THEIR LIVES, STEP INTO HOLINESS, AND STAY THERE.

Approaching God is exhilarating. It's completely ful-
filling. It's our identity. It's our lifeline, our survival, our
sanity. It's the joy of our heart and the light of our eyes.
Now that we've adopted the habit of getting sprinkled
with blood every morning, we're hooked!

It starts by getting a vision for living in the Holiest.
Then we make it a habit. The habit turns into resolve.
And ultimately, resolve can be upgraded to a pledge.

I've written this book to articulate a vision for living in
the Holiest. My prayer is that approaching God every day
through the blood of Christ will be your desire, and then
your habit, and then your resolve, and then your pledge.

Are you ready, yet, to make that vow?

> "Abba Father, I pledge my heart to get
> sprinkled with Christ's blood every day, and
> then approach You with boldness. I ask You
> to remind me to do this every day. My heart is
> loyal to the Lamb, and I pledge to demonstrate
> my loyalty to His blood by approaching You
> every day, for the remainder of my days."

Through the prophet Jeremiah, the Lord posed it as a
question. "Who? Who is this? Who is this who pledged his
heart to approach Me? Who is the one who is so loyal to
the Lamb that he pledged his heart to approach Me every
day for the rest of his life?"

"Us!" our hearts readily cry out. "We're the ones, Lord,
who have pledged our hearts to abide in holiness."

May His grace empower your walk until you have confidence to make this pledge; and may His grace empower
you to ever fulfill it. May *this* be the generation! May *this*
be the generation that rewrites our planet's destiny because they have abandoned themselves to living life in the
bosom of the Father.

Let's Get Sprinkled

Before closing this book, let's get sprinkled with Christ's blood right now. It doesn't matter where you are. You might be on a commuter train or doing laundry, it doesn't matter. Now is the right time to get sprinkled.

You may use the following steps as a guide. Let's go ahead and do this together right now.

Step One: Visualize The Throneroom

See yourself standing before the throne of God. God is seated on His throne, facing you, and Jesus is seated at His right hand, also facing you.

This is not an exercise in vain imaginations. It's actually very real. You truly are standing at the throne of God—it's just that you can't see it with your natural eyes. For now, you can see it only in the Spirit with the eyes of faith. Close your eyes if it helps you, and be reminded that you really are there, at the throne.

Step Two: Ask To Be Sprinkled

Simply say, "Lord Jesus, sprinkle me now with Your blood." And believe that He immediately does it. Receive His blood upon your mind, your conscience, your body, and your soul.

Lift your eyes in the confidence that comes with knowing you are perfectly righteous and accepted in the sight of God.

Step Three: Draw Near With Confidence

Now that you know you're being beckoned forward by God, draw near to Him in your heart. Wrap the arms of your heart around Him and cling to Him in love.

Say something personal to Him, such as, "Abba, I'm never letting go."

Step Four: Nestle Between Father And Son

The Father and Son are seated together in heavenly places, where the Son lives in the bosom of the Father. Make your way into the middle of their love-embrace.

Once you're there, turn around, and sit down with Christ in heavenly places. Visualize the Father now on your left, and Jesus now on your right. Snuggle into the bosom of the Father; then see yourself leaning on Jesus' breast. Enjoy this amazing union with the heart of God.

Listen to the love exchange between the Father and the Son, and let their affections resonate directly through your spirit. Ask to be included in their strategic dialogue, and also to participate in the execution of those exploits (Song of Solomon 8:6).

Step Five: Receive The Holy Spirit's Fire

As you look forth from your heavenly seat, you will see the Holy Spirit before you, burning with seven fires which are the seven Spirits of God (Revelation 4:5). Receive Him now into your spirit.

Allow Him to ignite you with the seven flames of God. Let the fire burn until you are aware that you fully one spirit with Him (1 Corinthians 6:17).

Pledge your heart, by grace, to stay here—awakened in love, burning in holiness, alert to His voice. You have found the place for which you were created. Let nothing move you.

OTHER RESOURCES FROM BOB SORGE

✣ LOYALTY is a fuller treatment of a subject that is touched only briefly in this book (Chapter 2, Loyalty To The Blood). Loyalty is a topic not receiving enough airtime in the body of Christ. This is truly an important book for this hour.

✣ SECRETS OF THE SECRET PLACE has become Bob's most popular title. Be enticed into the exhilaration of a personal, intimate relationship with the Savior. Practical insights will empower you to make the secret place a lifetime essential. Be sure to check out the Companion Study Guide.

✣ UNRELENTING PRAYER fuels our confidence that God will answer our prayer, which empowers us to pray without ceasing. Take a tender look at the issues of depression, reproach, and why God sometimes waits so long to answer our prayers. When justice comes *speedily,* you'll receive not only restoration but also seven-fold restitution.

✣ PAIN, PERPLEXITY & PROMOTION looks at the book of Job from a fresh, prophetic vantage. Job's life shows how God promotes His chosen vessels to higher heights than they would have conceived possible. Job's example is a template for God's end-time servants.

✣ THE FIRE OF DELAYED ANSWERS explores how God sometimes delays the answers to our prayers in order to produce godly character in us. This book is *spiritual food* for those in crisis or distress.

✣ IN HIS FACE propels the reader passionately toward a more personal and intimate relationship with Jesus Christ. This is blunt, straight-shooting devotional reading.

- ❖ EXPLORING WORSHIP is a 300-page textbook that covers a full range of subjects related to praise and worship. Translated into several languages, this bestselling book is being used internationally as a text by many Bible colleges, Bible study groups, and worship leading teams. Also available is an accompanying WORKBOOK/DISCUSSION GUIDE.

- ❖ DEALING WITH THE REJECTION AND PRAISE OF MAN is a booklet that shows how to hold your heart before God in a way that pleases Him in the midst of both rejection and praise from people.

- ❖ FOLLOWING THE RIVER provides powerful insights into how to follow the Spirit in corporate worship. This is essential reading for psalmists.

- ❖ IT'S NOT BUSINESS, IT'S PERSONAL: Jesus is not merely an entrepreneur who has found a promising enterprise on one of His planets. Rather, He is a ravished Bridegroom who has come to win the affections of a lovesick Bride. That makes it personal.

- ❖ OPENED FROM THE INSIDE: Taking the Stronghold of Zion: The taking of Zion is a gripping illustration of how you will penetrate, surmount, and overcome the obstacle that looms before you.

- ❖ MINUTE MEDITATIONS takes you through 365 concise insights that inspire meditation in God's word. Some of them will take seconds to read and hours to digest.

- ❖ See our site for a description on all of Bob's books. You can also order DVDs, CDs, eBooks (electronic books in .pdf format), and download free teachings. Visit us at www.oasishouse.net.

ORDER FORM
Books by Bob Sorge

BOOKS:

	Qty.	Price	Total
MINUTE MEDITATIONS	_____	$12.00	_____
OPENED FROM THE INSIDE OUT: Taking the Stronghold of Zion	_____	$11.00	_____
IT'S NOT BUSINESS, IT'S PERSONAL	_____	$10.00	_____
POWER OF THE BLOOD	_____	$13.00	_____
UNRELENTING PRAYER	_____	$13.00	_____
LOYALTY: The Reach of the Noble Heart	_____	$14.00	_____
SECRETS OF THE SECRET PLACE	_____	$15.00	_____
Secrets of the Secret Place COMPANION STUDY GUIDE	_____	$11.00	_____
Secrets of the Secret Place LEADERS MANUAL	_____	$ 5.00	_____
ENVY: The Enemy Within	_____	$12.00	_____
FOLLOWING THE RIVER: A Vision for Corporate Worship	_____	$10.00	_____
GLORY: When Heaven Invades Earth	_____	$10.00	_____
PAIN, PERPLEXITY & PROMOTION	_____	$14.00	_____
THE FIRE OF GOD'S LOVE	_____	$13.00	_____
THE FIRE OF DELAYED ANSWERS	_____	$14.00	_____
IN HIS FACE: A Prophetic Call to Renewed Focus	_____	$13.00	_____
EXPLORING WORSHIP: A Practical Guide to Praise & Worship	_____	$16.00	_____
Exploring Worship WORKBOOK & DISCUSSION GUIDE	_____	$ 5.00	_____
DEALING WITH THE REJECTION AND PRAISE OF MAN	_____	$10.00	_____

SPECIAL PACKET:

Buy one each of all Bob's books, and save 30%.
Call or visit our website for a current price.

Subtotal	_____
Shipping Add 10% (Minimum of $4.00)	_____
Missouri Residents Add 7.725% Sales Tax	_____
Total Enclosed (Domestic Orders Only/U.S. Funds)	_____

Send payment with order to: Oasis House
P.O. Box 522
Grandview, MO 64030

Name _____

Address: Street _____

City _____ State _____

Zip _____ Email _____

For quantity discounts and MasterCard/VISA or international orders, call
816-767-8880 or order on our fully secure website: *www.oasishouse.com.*

See our site for free sermon downloads.